TACITA DEAN

LIST OF CONTENTS

THE MARTYRDOM
OF ST AGATHA

(IN SEVERAL PARTS)

There are three known pairs of breasts belonging to St Agatha recorded in the Book of Relics. The first and most famous pair are on display in The Sanctuary of Relics in Venice. They are on show behind glass and have retained their form, but they are somewhat shrunken and brown and have the outward appearance of dried figs.

After her martyrdom in Third Century Sicily, Agatha's relics were carefully removed and packaged into caskets by the devout, before being smuggled to Constantinople. There is a rumour that the unfortunate Agatha met her ultimate demise at the hands of zealous relic hunters who were impatient for her death and frustrated when her mortal wounds were temporarily healed by St Peter. Unlike the miraculously preserved muscles on her limbs that were still in perfect condition on their arrival back in Catania nine centuries later, her breasts were mislaid. Stories tell of the growing reputation of their value as relics and their theft became inevitable. However some centuries later, they must have found their way back into the hands of the Church as they were recently discovered embedded in an altar when excavations took place above the small village of Nicolosi on the slopes of Mount Etna.

Stories tend to validate the Venetian breasts as the true and original upper part of St Agatha's body. However, the cities of Catania and Palermo dispute the authenticity of the Venetian pair believing their own duplicate sets to be the original ones. Catania's set are housed along with her sinews in an extravagant, bejewelled reliquary in the main cathedral and are never seen although the reliquary is paraded in February on her feast day.

The Palermo pair suffered greatly when they were taken hostage and the Church held to ransom by local terrorists. On their return, they failed to keep their shape and sit like two pyramids of dust behind reinforced glass in the city museum.

In 1669, there was a violent volcanic eruption and a deep crack opened up in the earth from the top of the village to the crater. Records talk of darkness falling over Catania and of horrendous shudders as columns of ash and burning stones were catapulted into the sky and blood-red lava began to flow in such abundance as to give the impression of a river of iron. The old village became entirely engulfed by a sea of lava and when it solidified all that remained to be seen above the black rock were the double domes of the ancient church of St Agatha.

A posse of monks and cardinals had tried to halt the lava flow by waving her veil at the on-coming stream, but it rose to sixty feet and prostrated the village as the monks hastened to safety. "For some time after this, faith in St Agatha's miracles suffered eclipse, but is now revived: as miracles only fail when the faith of the supplicants is not strong enough." When the solidified lava was eventually dug up at the end of the last century, the breasts were found in a gem-studded reliquary hidden in the altar table of the ancient church of St Agatha.

Let us pause for a moment...

Imagine you are standing in front of a painted altarpiece. You are high up, far away from the people gathering below. It is late afternoon and you are watching the story unfold. You stand in front of the central panel: the picture is completely contained and the narrative enclosed – you and the characters in the painting all look towards the middle.

You let your eyes survey the scene. You start on the left and are conscious of how your vision is being guided around the surface of the image until the path your eyes have taken has formed a perfect circle. You take in every detail: you look at their hands and the gestures they make. You look at the texture of their robes and the rings on their fingers. You look at the expressions on their faces – you become absorbed by their absorption. You see how beautifully they are painted: at the direction of the brushstrokes and the fineness of the detail.

You step back and see how the panel glows: how luminous it is: how the paint seems to have caught the light and held it there. Then you let your eyes wander to your left and to your right. You notice that on either side of the panel are two angels who lean into the centre and support the middle. Their faces are serene and their wings are golden. Beyond the angels on either side, is another panel, duller and further from the centre. Here stand the saints, three on one side and three on the other. They are upright and still and look out of the picture with unseeing eyes.

Each one holds something: an identifier, a memento through time of a temporal life, like a flower or an object or a part of their own body. You know you are being told a story and that each part is a cipher to the whole: that the saints are the prologue and the epilogue and the angels the supporting text.
You know too that it is the narrative of redemption and the saints are the human face and that the angels act as go-betweens, intercessors between them and the central panel, which is an allegory of heaven itself.

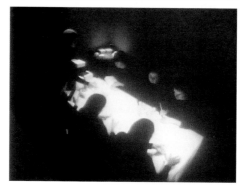

The Martyrdom of St Agatha (in several parts), 1994 (film stills)

7

You look back at the saints, at the blankness of their expressions – theirs is the story of real life: of sacrifice and devotion; of the implementation and consolidation of a burdensome spirituality. You look into their eyes: they begin to look smug, immortalised for their virtue in High Art. You begin to suppose sainthood to be the ultimate vanity.

At first the concept of St Agatha's "flaming virginity" was believed to be fanciful theory. However, recent carbon-dating has shown that her crotch was in fact alight and continued to burn with the Holy Spirit for many years even after her death. Of course this would have made any approach upon her person dangerous if not impossible and explains how she managed to maintain her purity despite the advances of the Roman Consular Quintian, and also helps explain how she survived her ordeal at the hands of Aphrodesia, the local brothel keeper, and her six daughters.

Its continued inflammation after her death also made it too hot for relic hunters to handle and they were forced to leave it behind. Eventually, it only stopped burning when she was finally beatified and canonised a whole century later.

The smouldering relic was at last interred in the crypt of the convent of St Agatha. A double dome was built to house two large bells that had been cast to commemorate her eventual resting place.

Nowadays, when the sun sets over the southern town, the bells call the faithful to contemplate her breasts and re-enact her passion.

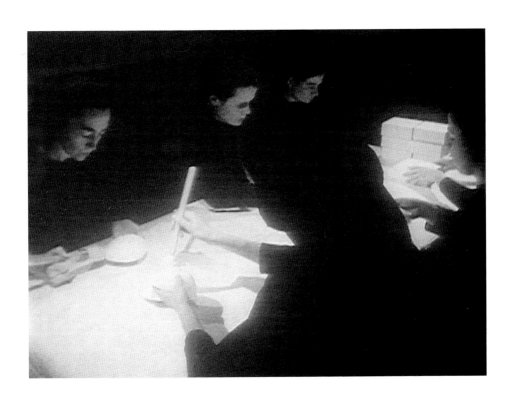

Above and overleaf: *The Martyrdom of St Agatha (in several parts)*, 1994 (film stills)

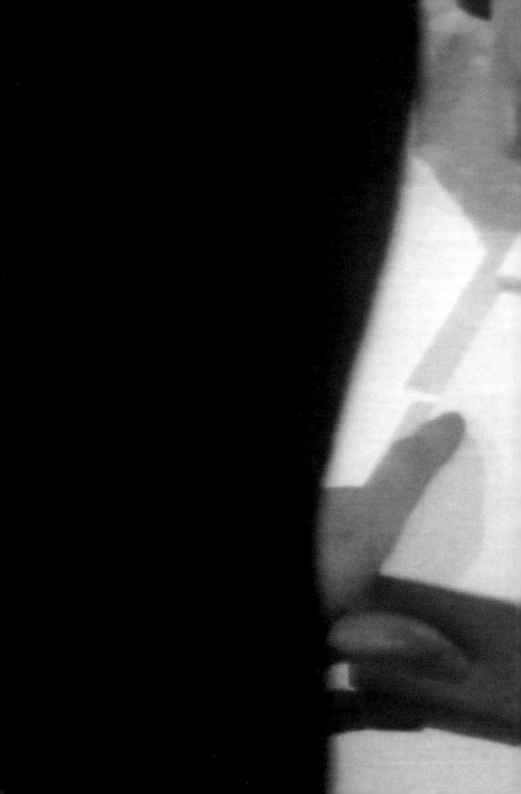

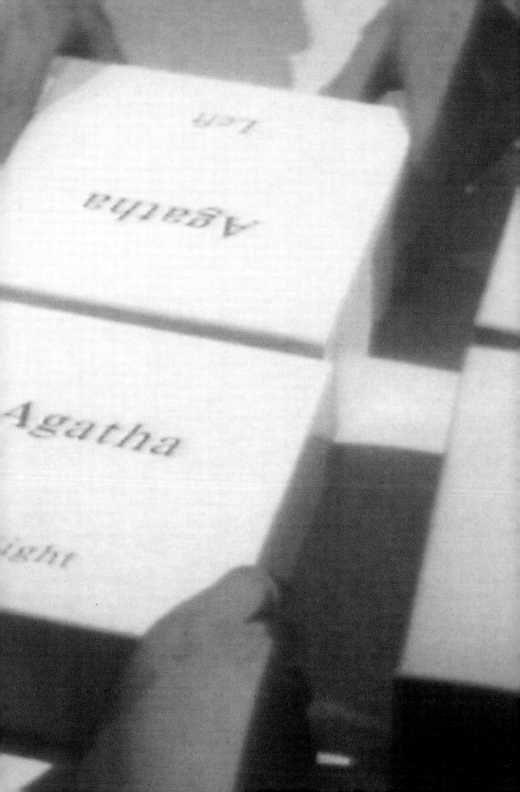

GIRL STOWAWAY

The story of the *Girl Stowaway* started with the finding of a photograph in a book. As I began to gather the information together to document her strange, illicit voyage from Australia to England, I embarked upon another more emotional journey, namely the travelling involved in the process of investigation.

Her voyage was from Port Lincoln to Falmouth. It had a beginning and an end, and exists as a recorded passage of time. My own journey follows no such linear narrative. It started at the moment I found the photograph but has meandered ever since, through unchartered research and to no obvious destination. It has become a passage into history along the line that divides fact from fiction, and is more like a journey through an underworld of chance intervention and epic encounter than any place I recognise. My story is about coincidence, and about what is invited and what is not.

The remarkable thing about her journey is that she did it all; that she actually undertook to hide in the hold of such an awesome ship as the Herzogin Cecilie one evening while on holiday by the sea. My journey has been less deliberate, and has become as much about allowing myself to travel this other strange and circuitous route as it has been about documenting her actual one.

"But this person who burst suddenly on us was a wretched young woman, thin, stragglyhaired, and seasick. She was dressed as a boy, and her angular figure aided the illusion. But she was more or less feminine. Her face was green, her nose red and long unpowdered, and the wisps of her mouse-coloured hair flicked in the wind like recalcitrant straws on a worn-out broom."[1]

My bag disappeared in an X-ray machine at Heathrow airport. I was on my way to Glasgow. That night I remembered I had packed the photograph of the stowaway. A week later, when they told me it had turned up in the hold of an Aer Lingus aeroplane in Dublin, I decided to find out if the stowaway had been on her way to Ireland.

"She asked one of the officers of the ship chaffingly where was the best place aboard to stow away. Without thinking that this information would be acted upon, he gave his opinion, and taking her courage in both hands she seized the opportunity of the dance to sneak into the hold, where she remained hidden for seventy hours without food or light and in terror of rats."[2]

Girl Stowaway, 1994 (film stills)

FAMOUS WINDJAMMER WINS RACE

THE HERZOGIN CECILIE REACHES PORT IN 96 DAYS

STOWAWAY ABOARD

The residents of Falmouth gathered yesterday at the Beacon to witness the arrival of the magnificent four-masted windjammer Herzogin Cecilie as she sailed triumphantly into port after 96 days at sea.

She came in under full sail and dropped her anchor in the middle of the Bay, and as the sun went down last night she could be seen like a museum model without its glass case, outlined against a silver grey sea, her splendid tall masts pointing at a fog encloaked sky.

The Finnish Herzogin Cecilie had collected her cargo of wheat in Port Victoria, Australia and had challenged the Swedish barque, Beatrice to a race. The Swedes put up the prizes and off they sailed. On reaching Cape Horn, the Herzogin Cecilie had not had sight of the Beatrice for four days and suspected that they had run into unfavourable head winds or ice bergs off the Cape.

The Herzogin Cecilie had an exceptionally fine run and not one storm during the whole voyage. Other boats in the race included famous Falmouth visitors, the, C. B. Pedersen and the Archibald Russell.

Captain de Cloux said, in his broken English, that he was delighted about the winning and that the Herzogin Cecilie was an exceptionally fine barque. He went on to describe how she came to be a Finnish vessel. After the war, as part of a reparation agreement a lot of boats were handed over from Germany to France and in 1921, while on his way to Marseilles he had arrived in Ostend and had seen her, quite by chance, laid up apparently hopelessly and on offer for £4000 and so he bought her on the spot.

Captain de Cloux said that he and his crew would be accepting the hospitality of the people of Falmouth and would be celebrating their winning in the Chain Locker tonight. His 23 person crew consisted of 18 Finns, 4 Danes and a mysterious young woman from Australia.

The captain told the story. After 3 days at sea, a boy appeared up from the hold. They were used to stowaways in the Australian trade. Last year a Norweigan whaler had 19 of them. It has become a serious thing and punishable by imprisonment. We believe he must have hidden in the hold while the ship was being loaded with cargo at anchorage. It is very dangerous and practically impossible for anyone except the stevedores to be aboard ship at this stage.

Girl stowaway in the "Herzogin Cecilie"

He begged to be allowed to work for his keep. I had no choice but to let him help in the kitchen and scrub the decks, because his build was so slight. He was a good-humoured chap and kept us entertained with long stories about life in Australia and even taught the crew some English.

One day after a scuffle in the washhouse, the boy turned out to be a girl. At first some of the crew became superstitious: women at sea are bad luck: women, and parsons and dead bodies in that order, but as days past with favourable winds and fine weather, gradually they began to relax.

She told us her hope was to get to Dublin and stowing away was the only possible means of her passage. She believed her grandparents to still be alive there.

The stowaway, whose name is Miss Jean Jeinnie of Port Victoria, Australia seemed content in the company of the crew. She said she intended staying with the Herzogin Cecilie until Ipswich where she hoped to get a passage to Ireland. She said she had kept a diary of her adventures which she hoped to publish under the title, 'The Log of the Happy Girl'.

FALMOUTH HOSPITAL

RECEIVES £2,285 FROM WEEKLY CONTRIBUTION SCHEME

Executive Committee, Mr. W. E. Hughes, J. P., was nominated; and Mr. W. Burge was added to the Emergency Committ ~ Mr Pillar was r· electe' ir nd in I

FAI

STII

Wi and a su present meeting Men's (for gen

Mr sided.

The scented follows

In have to of two Pinhay whom miss. N ber of i treasur of hap well-k as one which glad to comm conva Marty missec and w back. are de throug more i of our H. M illness impro so far it has regarc sight able t big ex separa The c out ex are ex winner medal.. known very en contrac the Chi favour of still a e h

Their
now p

**Boy of
'first c**

A BOY
rapi
age was
yesterday
youth cou
Straker.

n and her blind
'insters in their
pital last night
.tacked by an
'heir home in
London.
aged 88, who
itensive care
kull, broken
. a collapsed
~ Phoebe, 84,
icial bruising

.ers

Stowaway slips security on Dublin diversion

Sally Lewis

H EATHROW AIRPORT staff dismissed claims last week of a security lapse after an item of hand luggage disappeared in Terminal 1.

Tacita Dean, a visual artist from London, was on her way to Glasgow when her bag, containing original research material and a rare photograph failed to re-emerge from security machines. She placed the bag on the conveyor belt for X-raying, walked through the arch and on arriving to reclaim it found her bag had disappeared. A week later, the bag arrived in Dublin airport, unmarked from the hold of an Aer Lingus flight from Heathrow.

Ms. Dean accused the airport staff of indifference after they seemed reluctant to search for her bag. "I was distraught; the bag contained an incredibly rare 1928

photograph of a 'Girl Stowaway' that was an important part of my work, and I was left searching the departure lounge myself, believing it was probably still there: it was so frustrating."

Concerned about the security implications of the incident, Ms. Dean's solicitors, Stephens Innocent have pressed the Airport Authorities for an investigation into the bag's mysterious diversion to Dublin. "We are worried that there seems to be no monitoring of who collects bags from the end of the conveyor belt after they have been screened. This means that bags are susceptible to being tampered with by third parties or stolen, especially with a view to current security risks with flights to and from Ireland."

The Airport Authorities regretted the incident but denied liability and confirmed that their staff were unable to

Photograph of 'Girl Stowaway'

personally hand back items of luggage as they emerge from the X-ray equipment.

It is be'
case in w
has bee
since the
Wales v
September
common l.
a boy und
sexual in'
After
hearing,
be nam
was ren
bail unti

Nev
....

**Ang
ing** ..

The P
proce
when
agreed
meeting '

Breast c
Most c
may
wit'

Murder case wife insists she loved husband

Newspaper clippings belonging to the installation *Girl Stowaway*, 1994-1996
Overleaf: original newspaper article, *The Guardian*, July 30, 1994

15

Police seek hiker in 'best lead yet' on clifftop murder

Lawrence Donegan reports from Salcombe

DETECTIVES investigating the murder of a hotel worker at a Devon holiday resort yesterday released a description of a man who was seen arguing with the victim shortly before she died.

Police sources said it was the best lead yet on the killing 10 days ago, which has shocked an affluent yachting community where serious crime is all but unknown.

Witnesses said the man had been walking behind Sandra Parkinson on a clifftop path overlooking Salcombe. One person said he appeared to have had a disagreement with her.

The man is reported to be aged under 40, between 5ft 10in and 6ft 2in, with light-coloured hair and of athletic build.

He was wearing drab shorts, a light polo shirt and walking boots and was carrying a ruck-sack. Ms Parkinson's r body was found in 3ft u growth near a National walk on Thursday last She had been gagged, rape strangled.

A 23-year-old Scot, she among thousands of y people who travel to the s Devon town in summer, its 2,000 population rises estimated 10,000.

The mayor, Peter How said the town catered for ent holidaymakers — b ters, stockbrokers, even stars — and their children wanted to get away from it

They spend the summer ing and sailing, living i many holiday homes disc tucked away in woodl overlooking Salcombe estu

"The kind of people come are those who don't amusement arcades, r pubs or loud music," Mr

John Taylor (left) says Ms Parkinson was a perfect employee; below, the last place she was seen alive   PHOTOGRAPHS: MARC HILL

...aid. "They just want to sail ...boats, walk the country... ...or go to lie on the beach ...their family undisturbed."

...dra Parkinson, one of ...children of a working ...family from Stevenston, a ...seaside town south of ...gow, had gone to Salcombe ...york. She got a £100-a-week ...t the 14-bedroom Grafton ...r Hotel last year after ...ing to an advert in the ...magazine and the owner, ...Taylor, was delighted to ...her back this year.

...andra was living in. She ...d help out in the dining ...., assist in the bar, doing ...al housekeeping duties," ...id. "My wife and I grew ...fond of her. She was the ...ct summer employee — ...le, punctual, very quick ...rn."

...Taylor alerted police last ...esday after Sandra failed

to return for the evening meal. Like most hotel employees, she worked split shifts. She usually spent her afternoon breaks exploring the Salcombe clifftops.

Locals could not hide their shock when her body was found less than 24 hours later. "You just don't get crime in Salcombe," said Tim Walstenholme, a Humberside university student working at a town-centre cafe for the summer.

"The only thing you do get is people coming down from Plymouth to steal boat engines. You don't get burglary, stabbings or any of that kind of thing.

"Some people are saying that because she was dressed in cycling shorts and a leotard top, she was asking for it. But that's complete rubbish — Salcombe is the kind of place where a girl doesn't wear shoes or socks.

It's relaxed. For a girl to be

out walking on her own is perfectly normal."

Not surprisingly, Ms Parkinson's death has changed attitudes. "I have personally walked along the coastal path where she was murdered," said Jane Hughes, aged 24. "All the girls have taken to escorting each other around in groups. Salcombe is usually the kind of place where a girl can leave the pub on her own and not think twice about it. The worst you usually hear about is someone nicking a bicycle saddle."

But for older residents, the murder has revived memories of the town's most infamous mystery: the 1975 disappearance of a local mother and her two children. Police believe Pat Allen, her son Jonathan, aged seven, and daughter Victoria, six, were murdered. But the bodies were never found and no one has been prosecuted.

Then, as now, the difficulties facing detectives were compounded by Salcombe's ever-changing summer population. Police sealed off the town last weekend, stopping more than 4,000 vehicles. Meanwhile, detectives travelled to Sark — where Ms Parkinson worked earlier this year — and Scotland to interview her friends.

Detective Superintendent Phil Pyke, who is leading the investigation, said yesterday: "Not only are we facing a huge turnover of holidaymakers but we have a big holiday employment population. We have also had to trawl camp sites, hostels and hotels.

"Fortunately, the residents are very emotive about the case. They want it detected — you have got the problem that something like this affects the reputation of this place."

I was in a shop photocopying the newspaper article about the wreck of the Herzogin Cecilie when *Jean Genie* came onto the radio. So I went into town and bought the record. That evening I was having supper with an old French friend of my god-mother's. He told me that his name, Genet, like Jean Genet's meant "broom", the yellow flower you find by the sea. "And there is a lot of broom in Corn-wall," he said, getting into the spirit of coincidence.

Postcard showing the Herzogin Cecilie wrecked in Starehole Bay, May 1936

"Women seemed to be linked up with the Herzogin Cecilie. In 1928, an Australian girl, Miss Jean Jeinnie, stowed away on her and dressed up as a boy, later publishing a diary of her adventures entitled, *The Log of a Happy Girl.* "[3]

We were sitting on deck sailing out past the Dodman, imagining how Cape Horn must have seemed to the crew of the Herzogin Cecilie, when a huge and monumental cloud, the shape of a mountain, rose above the Cornish headland like nothing anyone had ever seen.

"For sixteen days, luck seems to have been against the Herzogin Cecilie for she encountered fog, calms, heavy rain and adverse winds. She was forced southward past Campbell Island until 55° in South and found at last her good west wind and started the Eastward drive to the Horn. By common consent, the bad luck had been attributed to the presence of a woman stowaway who was discovered on the second day out."[4]

We arranged to meet at the wreck of the Herzogin Cecilie on a hot, windless day at low tide. It was a coded place to meet as we only knew each other as a result of my interest in the stowaway and the boat she had hidden on. We camped on a ledge above the submerged re-mains of the great ship, and got up early the next morning to make the film. We packed up the equipment around teatime and left for a swim in Soar Mill Cove.

Later, we found out that a young woman had been murdered in Starehole Bay that afternoon. She had walked past us both, and was possibly quite close by when she died. The police wanted detailed and separate accounts of our every moment on that cliff path, and we were forced to make statements about our first night together that we had barely made to each other. The following Saturday, a photograph of Starehole Bay appeared in *The Guardian* newspaper, with the wreck as just a mark beneath the surface of the water: its first national appearance since it sank there in 1936.

Starehole Bay, July 1994. (Photo: Tacita Dean)

"The Duchess remained in Starehole Bay as a grim reminder of Devon's treacherous coastline and as a curiosity for holiday makers for nearly a further year. Then once again, a south-easterly gale came back to finish the Duchess off. This time great waves tore her wide apart. Her proud masts came tumbling down to lay in the sea beside her, and she disappeared over night."[5]

1. Ian Villiers, *The Set of the Sails. The Story of a Cape Horn Seaman,* New York: Scribner, 1949.

2. Basil Lubbock, *The Last of the Windjammers,* Glasgow: Brown, Son & Ferguson, 1927.

3. *Lake's Falmouth Packet,* May 1936.

4. William Lenson Arnold Derby, *The Tall Ships Pass. The story of the last years of deepwater square-rigged sail, embodying therein the history and detailed description of the Finnish four-masted steel barque "Herzogin Cecilie",* London: J. Cape, 1937.

5. John P. Cresswell, *The Loss of the Herzogin Cecilie,* Artscape Publications, 1994.

HOW TO PUT A BOAT IN A BOTTLE

I was invited to write the previous text for the catalogue of the *Mise en Scène* exhibition at the ICA in London in 1994. My brief was to write about all the "coincidences" around *Girl Stowaway*. However, at the time of writing I was involved in the murder enquiry at Starehole Bay and my relationship to coincidence had become an uncomfortable one.

I deliberated anxiously in the few writing days I had about whether or not I could mention what had happened in Starehole Bay. Obviously the murder had totally affected my relationship to the work. The police had wanted to impound my footage as evidence, and David, the other half of the "we" in the story, had been the last person to see the murdered woman alive; had chatted with her on the cliff path when he'd gone back to fetch the rest of the equipment, and had walked past the man who was following her, the man who had killed her. He was the main police witness, and a suspect too, and I was his alibi.

I was flying to Czechoslovakia the day after I had been questioned in Brixton Police station. They had produced a map of Starehole Bay where I had to mark with a cross where we had slept, where we had filmed, where we had lit a fire. They showed me David's map, somehow it bore no relationship to my own.

I was staying in Prague in the tiny flat of a friend. I sat on the balcony trying to write the story of *Girl Stowaway* but the describing of the "coincidences" killed them, and the appropriation of the murder into my narrative felt voyeuristic and gratuitous. The weather was stormy. The ninety-year-old neighbour had fallen and had an extended black eye across her face. At night she would cry out for her mother, banging on the thin wall that separated us. By the time I left for Ljubljana, the man responsible for the murder in Starehole Bay had committed suicide leaving a full confession. It turned out that he too had camped that night on the cliffs.

I never could express the story of Starehole Bay within the narrative of *Girl Stowaway*. However, a year later, I worked with an old sailor from St Ives and a friend from Lamorna to build a model of the Herzogin Cecilie to put in a dimple bottle. The desire was very simple: to bring the boat back to life and seal up her story like a tableau or still by putting the cork in.

How to Put a Boat in a Bottle, 1995 (video stills)

GELLÉRT

I have had in my possession for sometime a postcard of *Der Jungbrunnen*, a painting by Cranach showing a square pool with a fountain in the middle. To the left of the painting, elderly and infirm women are being wheeled or helped to the edge of the water. Once in, they undergo a transformation and become young, nubile maidens who are helped out of the pool on the right of the picture by handsome suitors. This is the fountain of eternal youth, and for many years I wanted to find such a pool so I could re-stage this metamorphosis.

The walls of the steam baths in Budapest are covered with testimonials from people who have sought and found relief from innumerable ailments in the sulphurous waters of the city. The complaints are mostly of a rheumatic or asthmatic nature. I would go to the Gellért Baths almost every day of my stay in Hungary, and watch the old women sit together on the steps of the pool, moving their bodies slowly and making them work again in the warm waters, momentarily rejuvenating them in those few precious hours spent in the baths each week.

Gellért Bath, 1998 (Photo: Sabina Lang)

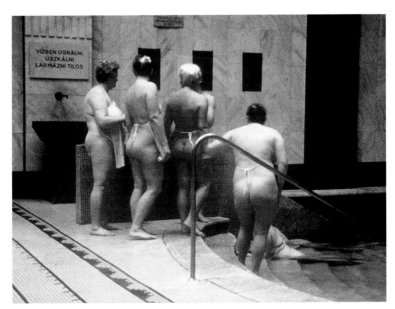

Gellért, 1998 (lambda prints)

A BAG OF AIR

CLOUDS   I remember wanting to catch clouds. I imagined leaning out of an aeroplane window and scooping them into plastic bags and sealing them up to take home. I remember the disappointment of my first trip, and realising that what I believed to be so possible, was in fact impossible. I think of this desire as being medieval; it has something to do with the visible and the invisible; with presence and absence. Clouds always look so present, but grasp at one and you grasp at nothing. I wanted proof of this presence, but what I didn't realise was that catching clouds was an act of faith.

I always imagine that Heaven must have become a much more complicated place to believe in, after humankind had learnt to get above the clouds. Suddenly we all had God's perspective on things, sitting up there in the sky, and looking down at the Earth below.

There is a small sculpture up high near the ceiling in the stairwell of Hôtel Lallemant. It is of a man blowing a horn, and from underneath him, it is possible to make out small cloud-like forms. I sought out the guide who knew of these things, and found her in the cafe Victor Hugo drinking coffee after a heavy Sunday's touring in the cathedral. She told me that they were indeed *nuée*, and that usually it was only angels and saints, and God of course, who were shown to be above the clouds. By having himself depicted above the *nuée*, the master of the house was telling us that he had reached another spiritual plane; that he had drunk of the elixir of life, and that now, he too, was eternal.

RAIN   It has been raining continuously today. I walked the wet streets to the Cathedral, and stood beneath the gargoyles as they spewed water onto the cobbles. They looked so human, salivating and dribbling like characters from a cartoon strip. I thought I might film them, and record that sound of water hitting the stone. I went and stood beneath the grand entrance, and watched the rain fall softly on the steps and seemingly turn to vapour. I thought about alchemy: the turning of substances with invisible meaning into something physical and tangible, rather like the faith that built this Cathedral, with the cipher to its construction encoded in its sculptures. So it is with alchemy, concealing itself deep within its process.

Palais Jacques Coeur, 1995 (photograph)

AIR   We made the rendez-vous for six the following morning, outside the church in Lans en Vercors. It was now getting on for six in the evening, and we were over 500 kilometres away with a daunting drive through the night. I had chosen Lans en Vercors because it was a region famous for its morning mist. I had made up my mind that I wanted to try and catch clouds after all, but from a hot air balloon. Discovering that no balloon will go up in the spring if there is any sign of cloud in the sky, I decided to simulate the experience with morning mist. Bourges being too flat to make mists likely, I had to seek out valleys, and hence the complicated juggling of windless, cloudless, misty weather conditions, and the last minute arranging of the dawn rendez-vous. As we neared Grenoble, the air got crisper and the mountains loomed. There was snow everywhere. In my provincial English thinking, I had not made the equation that valleys equalled mountains, I had imagined soft green hills dipping into the distance. As the sun began to rise, it became obvious that it was going to be a beautiful, clear day. In fact the clearest day that anyone could remember. It was a phenomenon, they all said. We always have mist in the morning in Lans en Vercors, said the butcher and the baker and the candlestick maker. So we rose on a beautiful morning, up high above the mountains, and caught fresh, clear air.

DEW The day we had risen to catch air was the same day that the alchemical couple would lay out their first canvas sheets to catch dew; they believed dew to be rich in the etheric essence of the forces of spring. I sought a definition for "ether", and found that it meant, "clear sky, upper air". There are four ethers: those that come up from the earth are the Life Ether and the Transforming Ether, and are found in dew. And those that come down from the Heavens: the Light Ether and the Warmth Ether, which are found in rain. By catching the dew and catching the rain, you are trapping the essence of all four ethers. Join the essence of rain with the essence of dew, and you are reuniting the four ethers, mixing an etheric medicine which will remedy disharmonies in the energies of the soul.

There is a small bronze credence, to the right of the window in a little room they call the offertory in the Hôtel Lallemant. Written across it are the letters "RERE", and then "RER". Above, on the ceiling amongst the many carved images, is a flaming ball, on which is written the inscription "3R". Fulcanelli tells of their possible meaning: "RE" means thing; so "RERE" means a double thing: a double matter; while "RER" means a thing and a half, and is the material of the vase in which one prepares the double matter. He does not mention what the thing is, nor the half thing. But as I gaze at the floating "R", I wonder if he could mean just that: that it is "R", as the French say it, "air", that is the mysterious, withheld element in this transmutation equation.

Hôtel Lallemant, 1995 (Photos: Tacita Dean)

TRANSMUTATION The birds arrived this morning, a Saturday morning right in the middle of July. The night before had been silent, peaceful: the sort of peace you do not notice until you lose it. I had never heard the like: a multitude of chattering; a dawn chorus tenfold, no, a hundredfold, all through the night, stopping and starting as if performing to some hidden intelligence. I watched them soar on the air currents, collecting in numbers as they disappeared overhead, and reforming to swoop down into the lime trees. And at some sudden point they were all gathered, and that was when they started their incessant conversations. One wonders at the content of their discussions, at the codes which make every bird on every tree silent, and then the invisible command which starts them all up again. When I returned in late August, they had gone; their absence now becomes more powerful than the memory of their presence.

I went to see a rheumatologist in Bourges. He came out of his room dressed like a surgeon with his gown tied up at the back. I asked him if he would mind quite simply just signing a paper. Yes, he did mind; he had responsibilities: *les cloches* would not allow him to do just this. No, he needed to know what paintings I liked, or did I prefer music. And what was my favourite instrument? He, himself played the French horn, you see, like the huntsman in his painting, and his receptionist sang in a choir. Please, I said, do you mind signing the form. No, he cursed, you need pills, pills are ''daddy'' and homeopathy is just ''mummy'': you need mummy and daddy. He knew a psychoanalyst who had studied in London, and who had told him that all the English were blocked. The paper, I said. No, he went on, slipping from *vous* to *tu*, it is like being on a boat when you cannot swim, the sea will get rougher and rougher, the boat will sink and they you will drown... It is the devil, he said, in all four corners of the room: in *that* corner and *that* corner, and *that* corner and *that* corner: you have to strangle him, he snarled, with something strong, like daddy, and not something weak, like mummy. Your parents should have smacked you... Please, the paper, I begged. Tch, he spat, you are a naughty little hare, I am going to pull your ears. And with his hand around my jaw, he pulled my naughty little ears, and asked if he could invite me to lunch.

A BAG OF AIR   If you rise at dawn in a clear sky, and during the month of March, they say you can catch a bag of air so intoxicated with the essence of spring that when it is distilled and prepared, it will produce an oil of gold, remedy enough to heal all ailments. And as you rise at dawn to the upper ether, and lean out to catch the bag of air, they say that you are trapping the ascending dew on its voyage from Earth to Heaven. And if you repeat this process each clear dawn for a thousand mornings, you will gather enough essence to fill a sealed flask and begin your manufacture. And in your flask will be a delicacy of substance that is both celestial and terrestrial. And if you separate the distillate from the residue each time and over many months, and until you reunite them at the end of your manufacture, they say you will have transformed your bag of air into a golden elixir, a preparation of etheric medicine capable of treating all disharmonies in the body and soul.

A Bag of Air, 1995 (film stills)

THE STRUCTURE OF ICE

Atoms are in constant motion; they touch and turn and move by mutual collisions and blows. And as they move, they collide and become entangled in such a way as to cling in close contact with one another.

And so it is with the hooked atom, it becomes involved with another atom into whose shape the hook fits.

And so too it is with the angular and sharp atom that is so formed as to produce a salty taste.

And those concave atoms that do join with those that are convex until they have all come together intertwining and clinging to each other, according to the congruity of their shape, size, position and arrangement.

And then they stay together to become compound bodies, until such time as some stronger necessity comes from the surrounding, and shakes and scatters them apart.

However, there is one atom that cannot be joined to another by hooking or collision or implication, and that is the spherical atom, of which the soul atom and the fire atom are composed. The soul atom is scattered throughout the body and is mobile because of its shape. It joins with fire atoms, which are also spherical, by the principle of like-to-like, by the use of a mutual bond.

Each fire atom grips the soul atom firmly, but at arm's length because of the bond, and each soul atom attends both the fire atom to its left, and to its right, vibrating to and fro as is its custom. And so this compound of three atoms joins together with a compound of three more, and so on and so forth, until it will produce the primary material that is the secret food of life. With fire as its father and soul as its mother, it will retain the qualities of both parents, mediating between them and reconciling their strife by virtue of its composition.

The Structure of Ice, 1997 (film still)

DELFT HYDRAULICS

We had to wait a year before Polish scientists with a grant from the European Community needed to use a wave machine. The Dutch no longer had a use for them and they stood to one side, "replaced" by the banks of computer screens and brightly coloured graphics showing the erosion of Venice by the sea. We were sent to meet them at their most northerly outpost in De Voorst, some two hours drive from Delft itself. It was a campus on reclaimed land: huge hangars down wooded tracks and false ponds with boardwalks. At lunch time, all the employees took a constitutional walk through the grounds. We would come across them in pairs or as groups as we drove recklessly around trying to orientate ourselves. The canteen, I remember, made me sad: it was a cliché of unfulfilment and routine, with pink and brown blancmange sprinkled with hundreds and thousands.

At the side of one of these hangars was the wave machine: elegant, functioning and full of rich green water. The Polish scientists, Mr Swidzinski and Mr Swieczkowski were standing in wellingtons carefully placing a lattice of finely attached blue marbles on a sloping surface at one end of the machine. A Dutch technician stood by. At some point when the laying out of marbles was completed, a signal was given and the pump turned on. A theoretical wave was sent down the length of the machine, picking up momentum and pushing the water into a perfect movement towards to the marbles. Throughout the afternoon, various shaped waves were sent along and their effect measured by the impact on the glue keeping the marbles together.

We went to De Voorst two days in a row, already getting the hang of things and a sense of the institution. The Polish scientists were beginning to frustrate their Dutch technician: you could sense he found their requests illogical and unscientific. Soon the last wave was sent down and the beautiful wave machine was drained of its green water possibly for the last time in its working life. We were told we had been lucky to see it working at all. We drove off the polder and back towards Delft using up the last reel of the film on a long line of modern white windmills that were turning on a still day.

Delft Hydraulics, 1996 (film stills)

ONCE UPON A DIFFERENT SORT OF TIME

THE STORY OF DONALD CROWHURST

Postcard with caption "Greetings from Teignmouth the Devon resort chosen by Donald Crowhurst as the home port of his triumphant around the World Yacht Race"

In 1968, Donald Crowhurst was one of nine competitors who entered the *Sunday Times* Golden Globe Race to be the first to circumnavigate solo non-stop around the world. He was a family man with a struggling business and no professional sailing experience, but his determination to enter and to win, set him on a path of delusion that swept up others and trapped him into leaving in an unfit boat, ill prepared and afraid. Crowhurst's story is as much about his bravado and the politics of a small provincial town as it is about epic voyages and heroism.

When you catch the train to what used to be called the Cornish Riviera to Penzance, you pass through a stretch of Devon where the cliff has broken away to form stacks along the coast, and the railway track borders on the sea. The train never stops at the station there, and is often moving too fast for you to make out its name. I was always fascinated by the thought of this place and I at last found myself there, because this was Teignmouth, the town where Crowhurst set out from, and his intended home port for the race.

I was looking for a postcard which I was sure had been produced to commemorate the event. I wanted some physical proof of the story: a token that would connect the man to the place. We went first to a newsagent but they had never heard of him and told us to try the docks. We wandered to a concrete jetty where a group of men were loading sand onto a trawler. I tapped the glass and asked a man in the security box. He told me to try Fred Tooley, who used to be on the Council. Fred Tooley was sitting in the dockers' cafe. He remembered Crowhurst very well, and thought he did have a couple of those postcards somewhere. If he could find them, and had two, he'd let me have one. We arranged to meet him later in a pub on the front where he was working as a bouncer.

We walked up to the Council offices: a house set in a park on the hill that looked out to sea. We had to start thinking about spending the night in Teignmouth and here were a row of bed and breakfasts that afforded a view of the docks.

Crowhurst's voyage was inextricably caught up with the affairs of Teignmouth Council. He became a tool for their Publicity Committee, and after he had found financial support for the construction of his trimaran locally, he named it Teignmouth Electron after the town. From what I can gather, he probably loved being the darling of Teignmouth in those few hectic months prior to his departure, but gradually this local pride became too much to bear, and in those agonising days when he was desperately trying to get ready to leave, he must have despised the bunting on the quay, and the dignitaries preparing to wave him off. They stood between him and his way of escape. He must have known there was no getting out of it then, and that he was trapped by his own bravado, and by their zealous civic pride.

I had been particularly struck by the closing paragraph in the book written on Crowhurst by the two *Sunday Times* journalists who had covered the race at the time. After they had reprinted the last few disturbing entries in his logbook and speculated on the manner of his death, they went on to report the minutes of a meeting of the Teignmouth Council Publicity Committee: "And his final verdict, as reported in the local paper, put the tragedy into the right perspective from Teignmouth's point-of-view. 'Despite the sad end,' Mr Bladon, the ex-Chairman of the Council, told the meeting, 'the voyage has brought up more publicity than this Committee has managed in fifty years. We have had this extremely cheaply, and I hope the town appreciates it.' Donald Crowhurst would have been glad to hear he did not die in vain."[1]

It is astounding with what ease they could pitch a man's life against the revenue brought into their seaside resort by tourism. The language they were speaking was wildly disproportionate to the hugeness of Crowhurst's ordeal and human failing. You imagine that if you met Crowhurst in the Teignmouth Yachting Club, you might find him a bit arrogant, but as a hu-

Berwick Lighthouse, 1996 (dye-sublimation print)

man being, alone in an unremitting seascape trying to come to terms with his deteriorating psychological state and his monumental deception, his story is genuinely tragic and existential, and leaves the aspirations of Teignmouth Council and little England way, way behind.

So we walked up the grassy slopes to the Council building, and were shown the musty ledgers from 1968 and 1969. Arrangements for welcoming Crowhurst home were neatly typed, point after point, in meeting after meeting: "4. That the Council provides hardboard lettering suitably painted for erection along the Point Car Park ('Teignmouth Welcomes Donald' was suggested). 5. That the Council erects its bunting and flags... 7. That Messrs. Honnor Marine be asked if they would permit Teignmouth Electron to be moored on their property on the night of arrival and transferred to the Lower Point Car Park next day into the custody of the 'Name it Teignmouth' Fund."

And later, after his abandoned trimaran had been found floating in the Atlantic and the real nature of his fraudulent journey unmasked: "The Council gave further consideration to the motion of Councillor A. L. Bladon that the Council agrees in principle to the boat Teignmouth Electron being brought back to Teignmouth and placed on show at an admission charge, the proceeds to be given to Mrs. Crowhurst and her family, and during the discussion on this item Messrs. Fisher and Parker were in attendance."[2]

Teignmouth Estuary, Devon, 1996. (Photo: Louise Short)

There was a small display about the event in the Teignmouth Museum. Yellowing newspaper articles mounted behind perspex, and bits of the boat purported to have been found by a local Teignmouth man who had come across the Teignmouth Electron in 1994, beached in the scrub on a Caribbean island. It had never been brought home after interest in the story waned, and was then sold off cheaply in the West Indies. The second owner swore he could still hear Crowhurst's footsteps at night restlessly pacing the deck. They had even found a stash of tins concealed in one of the hatches, only accessible from underneath the boat, so worried was Crowhurst of capsizing.

The Honorary Archivist, Nell Plahn, pulled out a manila envelope marked "Crowhurst" from her filing cabinet. In it were more newspaper articles and press photographs. She was sure there had never been a postcard produced. She showed us a painting by a local artist commissioned as part of the welcoming home preparations. The trimaran floated awkwardly on a ferocious blue brown sea. Crowhurst's disembodied head was painted in the right-hand corner amongst the waves. It was considered too inappropriate to have around after what had happened, and was eventually given to the Museum where it has stayed, out of sight, ever since.

We visited the local newspapers, and rang up the photographers who used to work for them, but no one had any original images, nor remembered the postcard. We went to all the bookshops, had fish and chips in a cafe in the main street and walked out past the pier and across the shingle to the channel along which Crowhurst must have sailed on his voyage out to sea.

It was getting on for nine, and time to meet Fred Tooley. No one else remembered there being a postcard. I began to worry there had never been one. The pub was a rowdy place on the front, and there he was on the door. He hesitated before pulling out an envelope from his jacket pocket. The postcard showed Crowhurst standing on the prow of the Teignmouth Electron. He was wearing a V-neck jumper with a tie, awkwardly formal for someone who spent his time around boats. He was looking down at the deck. On the back, it read, "Greetings from Teignmouth the Devon resort chosen by Donald Crowhurst as the home port for his triumphant around the World Yacht Race." Fred Tooley could only find one of the postcards and was reluctant to lend it to me. He eventually let me take it. He told us to go and see Syd Hook who lived in the last house in Ivy Lane. And to say that Fred Tooley sent us.

The sky was now sunset pink, but the curtains were drawn in Syd Hook's cottage. It stood next to the quay, and looked out across the yachts moored in the estuary. He didn't want to let us in. "Are you from the family?" he asked. "Are you from the family? Because I don't have a good word to say about him."

Syd Hook was working on the pilot boats when Crowhurst left Teignmouth. It was mid-afternoon on October 31, the deadline for departures, when he towed the Teignmouth Electron out to sea. But when Crowhurst tried to hoist his foresails, they were tangled and he had to be brought back in again. Syd said there was a sudden swell and his boat was that close to being hit by a rock, but they saved it. It was obvious to everyone that he didn't want to go. The boys down the yard said that the boat was just plywood. He must have known it wasn't up to it. Syd didn't think it would make it to Dartmouth, let alone around the world. He was amazed when he found out just how far it had got. "The man was a fool," he kept saying, his big arthritic fingers tapping the plastic table top. "Does he look like a sailor to you?" he asked, looking at Fred Tooley's postcard. "When we had to tow him in again, I said to his wife, if you've got any influence over him, you've got to stop him. She said she couldn't: there was nothing she could do."

Syd hinted at a conspiracy. I've heard this said since: that the whole trip was set up as a publicity stunt which went wrong. I don't know how far people will go, though, in implicating Teignmouth Council in the fraudulent records and the fake voyage. Syd Hook was convinced the whole sorry story had jinxed Teignmouth, and that the town had never been the same since Crowhurst.

Donald Crowhurst took 16 mm film, made tape recordings and kept logbooks. He got midway into the Atlantic before realising he would not survive one day in the Roaring Forties let alone make it around the world. Something happened here; rather than give up, he set about faking his journey. First by estimating mathematically his supposed position and faithfully recording it in a different logbook, and then by breaking off radio contact so as not to betray himself by continually transmitting through Portishead. He hung around the Southern Atlantic, avoiding the shipping lanes, and at one point, put ashore for repairs at Rio Salado, a tiny settlement on the coast of Argentina, which was against the rules of the race. After a while he just started to vaguely guess his sight readings and make more and more incoherent entries in his logbook, immersing himself in Einstein's theories on relativity and his own private discourse on God and the Universe.

Meanwhile, the world believed he was making great headway. His press agent in Teignmouth, Rodney Hallworth, became so exasperated with the radio silence, that he vastly exaggerated Crowhurst's progress. By June 1969, when Crowhurst's fictional journey collided with his real position in the Atlantic, and he could once again radio through Portishead, he learnt he was officially winning the race. The BBC radioed through arrangements to meet him off the Isles of Scilly.

But Crowhurst no longer knew where he was. He had lost all track of time and developed an obsessive relationship with his faulty chronometer, the instrument that measures Greenwich Mean Time on board. He began to suffer from "time-madness", a familiar problem for sailors whose only way of locating their position is through zealous time-keeping. Once his sense of time became distorted, he had no further reference point in the shifting mass of grey ocean. Overwhelmed by the enormity of his deceit and his offence against the sacred principle of truth, what he believed to be his "Sin of Concealment", Crowhurst "resigned the game" and appears to have jumped overboard with his chronometer, just a few hundred miles from the coast of Britain.

It took some time for Crowhurst's deception to be revealed. When they found the abandoned trimaran in the Atlantic, the newspapers talked of an accident, while Clare, his wife, believed he was still alive: "I am confident my husband is alive. I feel it."[3] When the logbooks were eventually examined, the anguish of his real journey was serialised in the broadsheets.

For many, Donald Crowhurst is just a cheat who abused the sacred unwrittens of good sportsmanship. But for some, it is more complicated than this, and he is seen as much a victim of the Golden Globe as the pursuer of it. His story is about human failing; about pitching his sanity against the sea; where there is no human presence or support system on which to hang a tortured psychological state. His was the world of acute solitude, filled with the ramblings of a troubled mind.

The Sixties were a time of exploration, of moon travel and experimentation, of pushing the limits of human experience. I do not believe anyone could have predicted what might happen if things went wrong: the flip side of success. At worst, the *Sunday Times* might have imagined someone getting killed trying to be the first to sail around the world, but not a death of such extreme isolation and distress. What happened to Donald Crowhurst was a cautionary lesson to everyone, but particularly to the press, at a time when adventure was being courted too casually, and probably went a long way in establishing what can happen at the very extremes of the human personality.

1. Nicholas Tomalin & Ron Hall, *The Strange Last Voyage of Donald Crowhurst*, London: Adlard Coles Nautical, 1995.
2. The minutes from a meeting of Teignmouth Council, 1969.
3. Front page of *The Times*, July 11, 1969.

Filming *Disappearance at Sea* and *Disappearance at Sea II*, Northumberland and Berwickshire, 1996.
(Photo: Ian Fairnington)

DISAPPEARANCE AT SEA

Berwick lighthouse sits at the end of the quay. The quay stretches out far beyond the town and far beyond the harbour into the water. As the train curls its way around the coast on its approach into Berwick-upon-Tweed, you can fix your eyes upon the dot at the end of the quay that is Berwick lighthouse and imagine the smallness of that enclosed space in relation to the vast immensity of the space beyond: the space that is the sea.

The lighthouse is the last human outpost between land and ocean and built around human scale. Nonetheless, its presence hints at the other worldliness of the sea: a different sense of space that will never be domesticated by humankind, and which is more akin to Crowhurst's final and distorted sense of things.

At night, you watch in the blackness for the rotations of the lighthouse and you decipher time in the gaps between the flashes. Without this cipher, there is no time. Crowhurst's "time-madness", where he believed he was floating through prehistory, utterly alone in an unforgiving seascape so far removed from human contact, is only just possible to imagine standing in the last human place where the ocean starts and the land ends in a solitary beacon of safety.

Looming in the window of the lighthouse, where normally the light would be, you can just make out the anguished face of Donald Crowhurst. Like the man in the moon, he becomes the light of the lighthouse, his gaze fixed eternally on the horizon as he looks out upon the sea.

Disappearance at Sea, 1996 (film stills)

DISAPPEARANCE AT SEA II

VOYAGE DE GUÉRISON

Poisoned, and on the point of death, when no earthly intervention could save him, Tristan surrendered himself up to the forces of the sea. He departed on a *voyage de guérison* – a journey of healing – where he floated alone in a small boat with no oars nor sails nor rudder. For seven days and seven nights he drifted at sea, guided only by the wind and the current, believing they would deliver him to a magical island where supernatural forces would heal his wounds and cure him of all ill.

His boat landed on the coast of Ireland, and the enfeebled Tristan was taken by sailors to the palace of the Kingdom of Gormond where he was healed by the unearthly powers of the Queen and her young daughter Isolde.

In the sixteenth century, a Portuguese governor was sent to India. During the voyage, he became ill and was struck by blindness. His flagship drifted away from the fleet and was guided by the wind and the current until it came across an unpopulated island in unchartered seas. The Portuguese governor gave the island his own name and called it Tristan da Cunha. To this day those shipwrecked in the Roaring Forties, off Inaccessible or Middle or Gough, build makeshift boats and try to make it to Tristan.

Becalmed in the Sargasso Sea, a sludge of a sea, thick with weed, where there is no wind or current, Crowhurst gave up his journey.

Disappearance at Sea II, 1997 (film stills)

TEIGNMOUTH ELECTRON

WINSTON MCDERMOTT   After its discovery by the Picardy, the Teignmouth Electron was taken to the West Indies and eventually auctioned off in Jamaica. It was bought by a man called Bunnie Francis who used it for one-day pleasure cruises in Montego Bay. He added a small keel to the main hull, took out the dagger boards and fibre-glassed the whole boat. He also built a huge main cabin to sleep ten people, and to house a calypso band. But, with the increase of crime and unrest in Jamaica, tourism fell and he was forced to sell the trimaran. It was then bought by Winston McDermott.

Winston McDermott had heard about the Teignmouth Electron from his brother. He had followed the race at the time and read about it in all the yachting magazines. He was fascinated by the story and borrowed the Tomalin and Hall book from a library before coming down from Canada to examine the boat. He bought it for $12,000 and sailed it to Grand Cayman to use in his scuba-diving business. Winston and his crew left in a tremendous storm and had to take the boat well south. With the modifications that Bunnie Francis had made, the trimaran handled beautifully during that trip, and better than any mono-hull the crew were used to. Their average speed was around 17 knots sailing close to the wind. Winston reckoned that with the small keel and the removal of the dagger boards, the underwater lee-boards attached to the floats that were designed to stop the trimaran blowing sideways into the wind, the Teignmouth Electron would have been the fastest boat in the race. Adequate sea trials might have resolved all these problems for Donald Crowhurst.

As Winston was a newcomer in Grand Cayman, and potential competition for the other local scuba-diving businesses, he had to employ someone to watch over the boat at night in case it got sabotaged and was cut loose and left to drift out to sea. He brought with him a Jamaican helper called Carl to sleep on board, only Carl was convinced the boat was haunted. One night he felt a hand holding him down as he slept; he lay there praying until it released him, then jumped overboard and somehow got ashore even though he couldn't swim a stroke. They found him the next morning on the beach, bitten from head to toe by sandflies and mosquitoes. He refused to set foot on board again and went back to Jamaica.

Winston also heard footsteps on the deck, but they never bothered him. After a while, none of his staff would sleep on board the Teignmouth Electron, so he would sleep there himself. He would lie awake at night and distinctly hear the feet pacing up and down above him. He would rush up on deck, but find no one there.

Eventually he took the boat to the smaller island of Cayman Brac where it got badly damaged one night in a hurricane. He hired a crane to take it out of the water so he could repair it, and bought a piece of land on which to put it. One day while drilling ventilation holes, he discovered four secret compartments full of emergency supplies which Crowhurst had concealed underneath the floats in case he capsized. He looked in two of them but everything had rotted away.

Winston never got round to finishing the replacement cabin and all the other things he intended doing to the boat. When he first laid it up, all the original charts and pots and pans and even the brass compass were still on board. But, over the years, it has gradually been stripped of all its contents, and now all that remains is the empty hull, and the basin and broken lavatory that lie on the ground beside it. Winston never goes there anymore; he has moved to Florida, and although his diving business is still in operation two minutes walk away, he can no longer bear to see the boat the way it is, rotten and beyond repair. He said he would never have it broken up despite the local pressure on him to get rid of it, and prefers to let it just sit there and fall apart in its own time.

Teignmouth Electron, 1999 (photograph)

CAYMAN BRAC   Until our discovery of the "bubble house" on the third day, the Teignmouth Electron seemed like the only bit of disrepair on the island of Cayman Brac. Everything else felt ordered and wealthy and fake. Our host in the bed and breakfast could not hide his contempt for our interest in the boat, and insisted on showing us his U.S. army service medals as alternative local and more worthy subject matter. He introduced us to an American woman who wrote for in-flight magazines because she was the one who knew all about "Winston's old boat", but we found her proprietorial and competitive, and more obstructive than helpful.

The island grew more and more claustrophobic, as we sat in our hire car waiting for one tropical storm after another to pass over so we could take the photographs. We drove along every road, and ate in every place, and then began to tire of Aunt Sha's kitchen and the same meal everyday, and the pervasive scent of air freshener. We sat hour after hour by the trimaran, with the airport timetables, waiting and watching for the moment when the plane was supposed to take off and fly over the boat. Only the wind would have changed, or something else had, and we would miss it again. In fact, that timetable, and our obsessive desire to photograph the boat with the plane, became the only structure in our day: it denoted when we could commence or abandon our vigil.

With the increasing humidity came the overwhelming desire to leave this strange and dislocated island, and a growing disquiet about its appropriateness as the final resting place

for the Teignmouth Electron. But in truth, where the boat actually is located on the beach does have a peculiar, if unresolved, dignity, sitting amongst the Coca-Cola bottles and the broken bits of coral, with the one solitary palm tree standing between it and the sea.

Teignmouth Electron, Cayman Brac, 1998.
(Photo: Tacita Dean, Kjetil Berge)

THE FLARES   After talking to Winston McDermott, I went back to the Teignmouth Electron and stood underneath the floats looking up at the secret compartments. There were four of them, two under each side, all tightly sealed with rusty bolts. I examined them, trying to work out which ones Winston might have opened. By the edge of the front left compartment, I noticed the wood had rotted away to leave a hole. I tentatively put my hand through and felt around. Inside, there was a distinct space, full of what felt like mulch. I carefully brought some of it out. In my hand was rust. I then brought out the remains of tin cans and disintegrated polythene wrappings, full of paper fragments. On one, I could make out the words, "lozenges" and "Slough". I carefully placed them on a wooden board out of the wind, and carried on. I groped more deeply into the space and felt a solid object. I started, thinking what it might be, and pulled out a packet of boatman's flares. There were three of them zipped tightly into a red plastic case with a transparent cover. They had obviously never been opened, and I could just make out the words, "PAINS BOATFLARES" through the yellowed front.

I brought the flares back to England and stored them in a film can. I later gave them to the National Maritime Museum for safe keeping where someone there, who knew nothing of their history, found them by chance and called in the Bomb Squad, who had them destroyed.

I tell this story because somehow it is significant. Crowhurst had hidden those flares in the underside of his boat because he was afraid of capsizing, in which case, they would have been his cry for help. He had never used them because that was not the cry for help he needed. The flares had to be destroyed because they were unstable and unsafe, and I should not have brought them back to England for this reason. But I did, and for some short time they were in the possession of the National Maritime Museum in Greenwich, somehow completing a circle in the cause and effect of Crowhurst's voyage, and the incorporation and perception of it in British maritime history.

Teignmouth Electron, Cayman Brac, 1998.
(Photo: Tacita Dean, Kjetil Berge)

49

J. G. BALLARD   Even before I found the Teignmouth Electron beached in the scrub on Cayman Brac, I had imagined it in the writings of J. G. Ballard. Now, as I walked along the road which ran parallel to the runway and caught sight of the trimaran in the undergrowth, more than ever did I place it in his fictional world, a world where the sea had retreated and left our boats stranded, or had risen and carried off our harbours to strange and unfit places. Either way the Teignmouth Electron was no longer in the right place.

J. G. Ballard summons up a time when our everyday will be out of context; when our descendants will read votive meaning into our sports stadiums and race courses; when nothing will be understood by the totems of today. I sent him an image of the Teignmouth Electron sitting among the bushes, and asked him what he thought about it. He wrote back in reply saying that he thought it looked a little like one of those Second World War crashed aircrafts that they were still finding in the jungles of Pacific Islands, which he supposed in a way the boat was. At other times, at other angles, it also has the look of a tank or the carcass of an animal or an exoskeleton left by an errant creature now extinct. Whichever way, it is at odds with its function, forgotten by its generation and abandoned by its time.

Teignmouth Electron, 1999 (photographs)

BUBBLE HOUSE

I went to Cayman Brac in the Caribbean specifically to photograph the boat of Donald Crowhurst.
It was the last stage of a long investigation into his
strange and ultimately tragic journey. The boat,
Teignmouth Electron, lay abandoned in the scrub on
the south side, rotten and beyond repair. On an is-
land that prided itself as a tax haven and a paradise
for the rich, the boat felt like welcome neglect amidst the neat housing and air-conditioned
world of the ideal holiday location.

It was on the third day that we decided to drive up the only other road on Cayman Brac.
On the same coast as the boat, "the hurricane coast", this road had fewer houses and ended abruptly in jungle. It was along this road that we found the "bubble house". Deserted, and
half-completed, the bubble house stood like a futuristic vision; like a statement from another age. We thought it was a temple belonging to a sect, or a church constructed by the
Mafia, with the faint imprint of a cross above the entrance. We knew we had come across
something otherworldly; the perfect companion to the Teignmouth Electron.

We frustrated our host by asking him about the boat and the "bubble house": both better
concealed, in his opinion, than on show on his immaculate island; both shameful relics of
fraud and deceit. "Bubble house" was the name the locals gave the construction, and it appears to have been built by a Frenchman. It was a vision for perfect hurricane housing, egg-
shaped and resistant to wind, extravagant and daring, with its Cinemascope proportioned
windows that look out onto the sea. Only he was arrested before it was completed; his as-
sets were frozen, and he was sentenced to 35 years in Tampa prison for embezzling money
from the United States government.

We were happy to spend our time passing from the boat to the "bubble house" and back
again, sheltering from the torrential rain in the rapidly changing weather. Nothing else on
that insular island took our fancy or held our interest. And the two were somehow connected: both men involved in their construction paid dearly for their fraud, and both boat
and "bubble house" seemed at home, if not altogether welcome, in their final Caribbean
resting place.

Bubble House, 1999 (photographs)

SOUND MIRRORS

DUNGENESS   Dungeness has always been a place of significance to me: a bleak pebbled peninsula where we would go as children across the Romney Marshes to get to the sea. Wandering along the shingle beach, I once found a huge stone that barely had any weight at all. I coveted this "trick" stone for sometime in my collection, and only writing about it now do I suspect that my discovery was more likely radioactive debris from Dungeness power station: lit up at night in the middle-distance, beckoning and repulsive, and perpetually humming.

The land around Dungeness always feels old to me: a feeling impossible to explain, other than it is just "unmodern". It is flat, scruffy and waterlogged, full of herons and curlews and Martello towers, and defences built against every threat from the sea this nation has ever known. To me it feels 1970's and Dickensian, prehistoric and Elizabethan, Second World War and futuristic. It just doesn't function in the now.

Close by, Lydd Airport still operates, serving cream teas in the Biggles Restaurant and shuttling people across the Channel to Le Touquet. I remember standing as a child at a gate when the airport felt more like a field, and looking at the big-bellied silver planes taking cars to France. Lydd Airport was the closest I got to air travel for many years. I could have been standing at NASA for the intensity of the thrill it gave me. Chris Marker's *La Jetée* makes me think of Lydd Airport. Something to do with the nature of memory itself: a black and white place full of tableaux and whispering and in this case, aeroplanes.

And then Derek Jarman moved to Dungeness and it became his place too. A home for his imagination and charisma, and for his film *The Garden*. I met him on a train just after its première in London, and he was on his way back to Dungeness. Mrs Thatcher had just resigned and everyone felt an enormous sense of relief. It was a heady experience for me to meet Derek on that train. I was studying at The Slade at the time and had a new life in London. I was going back home to visit my parents but felt estranged from my life there. Derek gave me back Kent, and Dungeness. *The Garden* was so full of possibility and magic and metamorphosis, that it created a new conceptual place as well as reclaiming the old one.

I went there the Saturday after Derek died, and stood in his garden amongst his driftwood sculptures and resilient plants watching the beam of the second lighthouse turn in the night sky. The power station twinkled; the shingle made huge banks down to the sea. Prospect

Cottage stood black and yellow under the vast sky, still full of Derek, readying itself for the icon it was to become. I walked from his garden to the road: there are no gates or fences in Dungeness: nothing to divide one property from another or from the beach itself. It is an empty desolate place, and I'm sure it is this desolation that makes Dungeness so utterly attractive: that in its emptiness it can become so full.

The Sound Mirrors, Denge, Kent, 1999.
(Photo: Mathew Hale)

DENGE   The sound mirrors sit like big ears in the landscape at Denge by Dungeness in Kent. When they were built between 1928 and 1930, nothing stood between them and the sea; and between them and France. Now the ground where they stand has been flooded and turned into a gravel pit. The mirrors have begun to erode and subside into the mud: their demise now inevitable. A caravan park separates them from the sea, and a barbed wire fence divides the mirrors from the holidaymakers and the weekend ramblers. To get close to the site at Denge, you have to trespass.

The sound mirror scheme was conceived during the First World War when the concept of an air attack became the new danger to national security. The development of an early warning system became a matter of great urgency, and detection through acoustic methods seemed one possible solution. A series of listening stations were developed on the South coast using diverse methods of sound collection. Six varying sized mirrors were built on three different locations. Listeners would sit in chambers beneath the concrete structures using stethoscopes to monitor the direction and strength of the sound. The idea was to catch the vibrations of planes taking off in France and to plot their course towards Britain, having first alerted London.

Only the mirrors were not discriminating enough. Although they caught the sound well, they would also pick up other noise, like the wind and the traffic and the propeller of a passing passenger liner, making any effective warning impossible. They persevered with them for a while, but soon they were abandoned in favour of the radar: an exciting new development with radio waves. An order to have them destroyed got lost with the outbreak of war, and these listening monoliths were spared and left to stand, solemnly eavesdropping on the sounds of Dungeness into the next century.

The Sound Mirrors, Denge, Kent, 1999. (Photos: Mathew Hale)

FERNSEHTURM
BACKWARDS INTO THE FUTURE

The Fernsehturm has become the beacon on my Berlin horizon. I look out for it wherever I am, in all weather, with its head so often lost in the low cloud or standing high above the city brilliantly catching the sun. I think it is beautiful; it excites me, yet so many people don't like it. Most Berliners from the former West have never been up it, yet large groups from the former East still book long in advance to have dinner in its revolving restaurant. The Fernsehturm has retained its political edge despite its consumption by the tourist world.

I went up it in 1986 on a college trip to Berlin. I remember the smell, the cloying cakes and the utilitarian atmosphere of this cafe above the clouds. But I loved it. I was told recently that in those days it took an hour to do a single rotation, and that that was exactly how long you were allowed to stay there for: one look at the full 360 degrees of the Berlin horizon and then out, never allowing for a second glance. There were not many public places to eat in the former GDR so a seat in the Fernsehturm restaurant was highly sought after. Consequently, it was one of the better jobs to work for the tower, so the staff were inevitably "approved by the Party". It now takes half an hour to do the full rotation. So with the progress of reunification, they have doubled the speed. And now you can stay as long as you like. But the staff, who are for the most part the same staff, still seem to work with the old system. Your order is taken and delivered with impeccable speed and efficiency. They move around the restaurant floor as if choreographed for the *corps de ballet*, never pausing to show disorientation or doubt as their world continually shifts and moves away from them.

Like the perpetual rotation of the spacecraft in Stanley Kubrick's *2001: A Space Odyssey*, a conceit to maintain gravity on board a ship, the Fernsehturm restaurant continues to turn almost imperceptibly like the movement of the planets in Space. It was visionary in its concept and a symbol of the future, and yet it is out of date. The Fernsehturm embodies the perfect anachronism. The revolving sphere in Space still remains our best image of the future, and yet it is firmly locked in the past: in a period of division and dissatisfaction on Earth that led to the belief that Space was an attainable and better place. As you sit up there at your table, opposite the person whom you are with, and with your back to the turn of the restaurant, you are no longer static in the present but moving with the rotation of the Earth backwards into the future.

The Fernsehturm, Berlin, 2000. (Photos: Tacita Dean, Mathew Hale)

FROM COLUMBUS, OHIO TO THE PARTIALLY BURIED WOODSHED

ROBERT SMITHSON   In New York, someone mentioned that the *Spiral Jetty* had risen, and that was enough to set me off on a journey to try and find it. Although it prefigured in my imagination as a black and white slide projected on an art school wall, it became an icon for me that summer; a virtual reference that beckoned me away from the unfamiliar but exhilarating world of the Sundance Screenwriting Lab. I set off with directions from the Utah Arts Council and a friend from the Lab. We took the I-80 north from Salt Lake City. He had no idea what we were looking for.

The journey to Rozel Point, more than any journey I can consciously remember taking, led me back into my imagination. I feel I often go there: to the primeval hill formation and

the thick red lake, where all the vegetation is covered with a 1/4 inch of salt and where the air at dusk is so full of mosquitoes that they sound like rainfall hitting the car windscreen. It has become a place of time travel, of prehistory and the future, of the sedimentation of thinking and the very matter and fabric of film.

Robert Smithson has become an important figure in my working life, not because I depend on him in any way, but because his work allows me a conceptual space where I can often reside. Artists don't talk about this very much, because it is extremely difficult to describe. It's like an incredible excitement and attraction across time; a personal repartee with another's thinking and energy communicated through their work. Looking for the *Partially Buried Woodshed* was about visiting one of Smithson's delegated places; one of his crosses on the map. Personally, I don't believe the woodshed is where Kent State University say that it is. I believe it is beneath the tarmac in the car park where you leave your car in order to approach the wooded mound described as "Earth Sculpture" on the campus map.

Contrary to current mythology, Smithson didn't want his works to disappear. In fact they are talking about rebuilding up the *Spiral Jetty* so you can walk along it. So it will have risen again, no longer submerged in some prehistorical state in the Rozel Point of my imagination.

From Columbus, Ohio to the Partially Buried Woodshed, 1999 (video stills)

FOLEY ARTIST

I worked with Beryl and Stan down at Shepperton Studios to make *Foley Artist*. Beryl had been in the trade for years. She started as a child star, but somehow ended up in foley. She still carries herself like a screen star, even though she is never seen in the films she makes. We can hear her though; once you meet Beryl, her stage presence is unmistakably there.

Everyone knows her. The boys in the business call her "Beryl the boot". When I rang to ask if she would be my foley artist, she told me that she'd been busy all week doing ants for David Attenborough. Because she's in her seventies now, her timing is a bit off so the studios don't use her as much. She gets more Variety type foley work like nature programmes, children's workshops and a "show us how it's done" for Michael Aspel. When I said I wanted two artists, she said she'd bring Stan.

Stan is known as "Stan, Stan, the footsteps man". He told me he'd been Miranda Richardson kissing Rupert Everett and the ape at the beginning of *2001*.

It must be a strange relationship to cinema, to never let yourself be taken in by the fiction of it all: to go to the movies and listen to the foley, where the cinema kiss is always only a measure of your trade's expertise and each footstep a matter of professional competence.

"How did you do the sound of the ape with the bone, Stan?"

"Oh, we brought in a dead pig and hit it with sticks, Tacita."

Foley Artist, 1996 (video stills)

FRIDAY / SATURDAY

HOONAH, ALASKA We had to learn to judge a place by its sound. Dixie D's Snack Bar seemed to block out the hum of the canning factory's generator that carried everywhere else through Hoonah. In fact, we only ended up there by chance. In our mad dash to find somewhere to record, Sandy, our impromptu guide, had fancied a cappuccino and the porch of Dixie D's, situated next to the harbour and at the social centre of the town, became our chosen Alaskan location. Our intention had been to record the sound from an uninhabited island which lay dead on 135° W, where, we'd been told, we would hear whales mating and the crying of bald-headed eagles. However, we had no "bear training", and Mike, our pilot, was reluctant to leave us there, feeling sure we would probably be incapable of shooting a bear in the nose if she was charging towards us. There had been a mauling recently, and the sight of a fresh bear print in the sand made it feel like the right decision. We had also missed the whale season. So we slept in recliners in the steel interior of the snack bar kitchen, ceremoniously changing the tape every two hours, and monitoring the dawn arrival of fishermen impatient for their first coffee of the morning.

NEW ORLEANS, USA In New Orleans we chose the bandstand. Rather we took shelter there from a torrential rainstorm that moved across the Mississippi and emptied the riverwalk in minutes. The place should have been buzzing. Instead it was deserted, but for a couple of homeless men and a busker who were also sheltering there. And then, with little sign of a let up in the weather, they too were gone and it was just us, sitting it out, on the Friday afternoon before Memorial weekend. We watched the lightening, and the riverboats with their empty decks, and some blue balloons blown onto the surface of the river get consumed by it. A quartet of figures in matching pink kagoules bravely set out and then retreated. A water rat ran across my foot and I screamed. New Orleans felt bleak. And then the rain lessened. The Mississippi steamboat took a deep breath and began blowing its overture, and people appeared from nowhere moving towards it in the hot damp air. The buskers returned to their spots, got out their instruments and began replaying their tired limited repertoires, and the homeless returned to the bandstand.

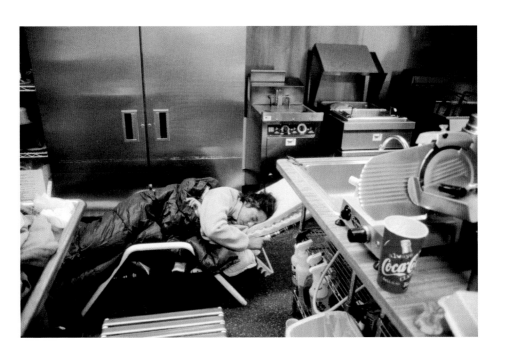

Dixie D's Snack Bar, Hoonah, Alaska, Early Hours of the Morning, 2000 (photograph)

NASELESELE, FIJI   We chose Naselesele because of Meme. She told us to find some good kava for the presentation, and then arranged for Mathew to meet her chief, who gave us the protection of his village. We set up in the corrugated iron meeting hut, and Meme brought us bedding and mosquito nets. The village went to bed early. But we were woken by the arrival in the hut of some musicians who had been playing in one of the beach resorts. They sat in a circle and sang one song. I lay under my net listening to their sound: it was such a beautiful song, full of Fiji and the South Pacific, and of the romantic elsewhere. And then they began to drink kava and invited Mathew to join them. Every time one of them drank from the half coconut, they would all clap three times and pass it onto the next man. And after they had all drunk once, they would sing again and so it continued until late into the night for some eight or so songs, and some eight or so rounds of kava. By the time they left, it was raining hard onto the corrugated iron roof of the hut, drowning out the sonorous cicadas that had been background to the musicians. Mathew fell into a deep kava induced slumber and I lay awake, listening and remembering that late lost song.

ADEN, YEMEN   We rejected the main souk because there was just too much noise and went back to the Qat market in the Port district of Aden. The little square resonated with sound because of the mountains behind it. We left the microphone on the roof of Cafe Alshabani, and took up various places of vigil. At dusk we sat on the iron beds of the Qat sellers who sold the shrub in cheap coloured plastic bags. We had noticed the bags everywhere blowing empty in the vast desert landscape, and had wondered what they could possibly be. And now we realised that the plastic bags were the detritus of Yemen's addiction to chewing Qat. So we chewed too, with Firas, our guide and Waleed, our Ministry of Information official: their cheeks bulging with hours of mastication. Soon the Qat sellers wanted to pack up and we had to leave the beds. Throughout the night, the four of us played pontoon in Abu Talal's cafe which seemed to want to stay open. With the coming of dawn, the square filled with the morning call to prayer and the howling of dogs in the hills, and then the crows. Altawahi souk was full of crows. And then there were a few more people in the square. The taxi drivers who had been sleeping on their car roofs in shrouds like corpses began working again, hooting at the kid goats left to wander and at the people setting up for the day. It got hotter, and was all as it had been the day before when our recording began.

Waleed, Our Ministry of Information Official, Yemen, Early Hours of the Morning, 2000 (photograph)

Altawahi Souk, Aden, Yemen, Early Evening, 2000 (photograph)

Qat Sellers, Altawahi Souk, Aden, Yemen, Late Evening, 2000 (photograph)

BANEWL

On location for *Banewl*, Burnewhall Farm, St Buryan, Cornwall, 1999. (Photo: Richard Torchia)

It is raining as I sit in the bottom field, waiting. The weather looks set in. There is a permanent roar from the BBC's Hercules plane as it films high above the clouds: the eye of the nation seeing above the gloom what we cannot see from below. As the time ticks away to totality, the light still feels remarkably unchanged. The swallows perceive the darkness coming long before us. Suddenly they go crazy, swooping and darting in all directions, and then they disappear. The cows start to lie down one by one across the field. The temperature drops.

When totality comes, it is rapid: a night darkness. The sun gone. There is a mustard yellow horizon, the light from beyond the furthest edge of this shadow moving above us. And this is what is changing, turning from strange translucent colours to mother of pearl and then imperceptibly back to grey: the grey that is normality; the grey that is today's weather. There is a cheer from Logan's Rock. Still in a reverie, seeing the world again, but now in the context of the extraordinary, the silence is eventually broken by the crowing of the cockerel: its blood red throat signalling relief, and the passage from one phase of this phenomenon to the next. Twenty minutes later, and we are well into the "anti-climax" of this event. The sun starts to show through the clouds for the first time. People on Porthcurno Beach are packing up their things and going home. Through filtered glasses the sun has become like a crescent moon. The eclipse is again about waiting and watching until the sun becomes whole again.

I cannot quite explain the madness that took hold of me later that night. I wasn't on my own: Dick, my American friend sat in his armchair, exhausted, giggling hysterically with both delight and disappointment. We began to see the sun in everything: in a brass plate on the wall; in some frieze decoration in the farm's sitting room; in the bare electric light bulb. Watching the footage from the Hercules on the late night news and reports of the eclipse from around the world, I felt jealous. I couldn't even tolerate seeing the sun in the sky in some incidental and unconnected report from Australia. It is beyond rational explanation, but for some short time after that day, I really felt like I would never recognise the sun again.

But the clouds had given the day a strange intensity. We hadn't seen the sun's corona nor the diamond ring effect, and Dick hadn't found any crescent suns pinholed beneath the trees. What we had was the place: the ground and the sky; the animals and the birds, and Banewl, the farm itself. The eclipse was about waiting for darkness to happen and then equally for the return of a normal sun. The clouds allowed us to experience this coincidence of cosmic time and scale on our terms and in our own human time, measuring it against the movements of animals and the fine detailing of our natural world.

Banewl, 1999 (film still)

Banewl, 1999 (film stills)

Banewl, 1999 (film still)

TOTALITY

You're looking directly at the sun; it is all but entirely covered. Suddenly the moon seems to lurch across it, and the sun is gone. For two minutes and six seconds there is nothing; just blackness: it is like watching, rather than waiting for the two minutes of silence on Armistice Day to take place – only they seem to pass more quickly: six seconds more quickly, maybe, but they feel over in a flash. This seems to last much longer, probably because it's more difficult to perceive the actual end of this darkness.

And then eventually the moon sidles across, and reveals the sun again. Slowly there is more light, incrementally: so incremental, in fact, that it is difficult at first to believe in that minute shift in tone which just draws out totality longer. And then you really can see a lightening of the sky. The moon moves to reveal more of the sun. After eight interminable minutes, 10% of the sun is exposed, and the light is already normal again. A bird then flies across the picture frame and shifts the plane of concentration.

Totality, 2000 (film still)

COLLECTIONS

When I was about eight years old, I went for a walk up the lane behind our family house in Kent. I was probably imagining, as I often did, that I was in a documentary, in dialogue with an invisible camera, talking about horticulture or some other such worldly subject, when I came to a lay-by beside the road. Looking down in amongst a clump of grass, I found my first four-leaf clover. Further visits to the same lay-by harvested a full eight four-leaf clovers. So I wrote to *The Guinness Book of Records*, only to receive some while later a letter with the printed signature of one of the McWhirter twins. It told me that the largest quantity of four-leaf clovers had, in fact, been found by someone in Ohio, and that the record was in the thousands. Indeed, it continued, such mutation in nature was not at all unusual.

Undeterred by the official response to my discovery, I found I had a "facility". Whether it was a good eye for a clover or "good luck", I would find four-leaf clovers wherever I looked and where others couldn't. I would see one crossing a lawn or walking along a road. I would notice it, stop, pick it with care, check for others, because where there is one there is often another, then press it in my notebook. At some future point, I realised I had a collection.

Now, the problem with a collection is realising you've started one. Recently, I have begun, quite unintentionally, to collect old postcards *thematically*. It started with finding an attractive postcard of a frozen water fountain. On finding the second frozen water fountain, I had begun a collection, although I could delay acknowledging it as such by choosing to call it a diptych, or a triptych, or a quartet. And so it is with postcards marked with crosses, by a hotel window or a table in a restaurant or a mountain climbed, or postcards showing seagulls or thermal spas or four-leaf clovers. All my interests in microcosm: portable, collectible, reproducible.

I know people whose lives are dominated by their collections, ceaselessly searching in flea markets, auction houses and specialist book shops, never resolving their quest. Whether you are collecting versions of popular songs, postcards of lighthouses or votive sculptures of Our Lady of Montserrat, your collection will never let you be. You've started so you must continue, and with most collections, there is no end. Whether it is postcards of lighthouses or four-leaf clovers, there can never be the definitive collection. For what is more inert than a finished collection?

What happened to me and my clover collection was that it became an investigation into my relationship to luck. I had always courted Chance, and the ease with which I found four-leaf clovers made me too sure of this special relationship. When I first showed my collection in 1995, for the first time in my collector's life, I became paralysed by an inability to find any more four-leaf clovers. It was as if I had turned the accidental action of finding a clover into something altogether too self-conscious. I had played an uncomfortable game with Fortune and She had shunned me for my ostentation. I suddenly searched too hard and could no longer find.

My clover collection is not a dead collection, although its constituent parts are dead. No, because I had to surrender it and let it go, and stop my obsessive searching of grassy verges and uncut paddocks, I have at last now managed to re-find something of my ability to chance discover and to find by not looking. And I can now add, from time to time, a new clover to my collection.

A CONVERSATION
WITH TACITA DEAN

ROLAND GROENENBOOM

I see a shift in your films from the earlier ones that have a spoken narrative, such as *The Martyrdom of St Agatha (in several parts)*, *A Bag of Air* and *The Structure of Ice*, to those from *Disappearance at Sea* onwards. From this moment you are no longer using spoken narratives anymore.

There was a shift around *Disappearance at Sea* which became about leaving the narrative off. When I made *Disappearance at Sea* I actually had intended to put a narrative on it. But what happened is that the footage was absolutely self-explanatory. It did not need me to say anything. So that was the moment I abandoned the spoken narrative. I do not say that they are totally non-narrative, as they always have beginnings and ends and there is always an event. In *Disappearance at Sea* the event is the passage of time, going from light to dark when the lighthouse becomes functional. For *Teignmouth Electron*, for example, the event is an aeroplane taking off. Or with *Bubble House*, it is a storm coming in from the sea. There is always an event, so they are narrative, they are events in time. You cannot encounter them and leave like you can with some artworks. They do require the viewer to spend the whole time there in order for them to make sense. It is a different definition of narrative. What happens is that often the narrative is running parallel to the film, but it is not on the film. It does not describe the film, but I write an adjacent story which exists as a separate entity. It sits side by side with the film.

Since the spoken narrative is not there anymore, sound seems to have gained more importance. In recent films, the shots are longer and more static, but at the same time the construction of sound plays a more important role.

Yes, it does. The sound describes the event. It is funny how I use sound. I never make films with sync sound. In fact the only time I have done that was with *The Martyrdom of St Agatha (in several parts)*. My sound is more random than that; it is always just ambient sound. Then I manipulate the sound for the film. This happened especially with *Banewl* which took it to extremes. The construction of the soundtrack was as detailed as the construction of the image. It has an equal status in the film. In that sense it totally describes the film, as much as the image does. For example, there was a Hercules aeroplane flying above Cornwall, backwards and forwards above the clouds, filming the eclipse for the BBC, which was being transmitted live. And that makes an incredibly ominous sound. When I was actually filming I was not aware of it. Only when I listened to my sound did I notice that this totally dominated it. It described the atmosphere and did it very well in a way. What people do not realise is how much sound in cinema is constructed anyway, which is what *Foley Artist* is about. With *Banewl*, every bird that squeaks, every sound is constructed after the event.

In *Sound Mirrors*, you hear lots of different sounds, from birds to aeroplanes. Was this totally constructed or were they the actual sounds recorded through the *Sound Mirrors*?

The thing about the *Sound Mirrors* is that they were built in between the First and the Second World Wars at a time in which aeroplanes became a threat. They were meant to be used to trap the sound of an enemy aeroplane approaching from France, like an early warning system. Why it failed is that they could not discriminate between the sound of a propeller in a boat passing on the sea and the sound of an aeroplane coming. They were also non-directional in a way. Now they are in a flooded area, a sort of nature reserve on private property. In terms of the nature there it is extraordinary. You have seabirds and waterbirds. But what is so special about the mirrors is that they do trap sound in a very effective way. So what I did is to record all the sound in the 200-foot wall. You can actually hear a pin drop, the sound there is exquisite. Rather than using sound as a conventional narrative filmmaker might, using it in such a way that as soon as you would step behind the 200-foot wall you would not hear the sound, I actually used the sound throughout the film, like "this is what they were hearing". This is what the sound mirrors hear. Rather than making it a kind of human thing, for example. What a spectator would hear, were they standing behind the wall, would not be those sounds. I used that soundtrack to make it more vivid. What is so beautiful about that area is that it is a very old area of Kent and a place I know very well. You have the Romney and Hythe & Dymchurch Railway and you have Lydd Airport, so you have all these other things going on there, kind of old sounds. It is not only the marsh birds, it is also the aeroplane and the little leisure steam train. What I like most about this film, and this is how I figure if it is being shown properly or not, is if you can hear the motorbike at the very end of the film. Some young kid just driving around and around on a motorbike. That for me is such a particular sound of England, or maybe Europe, in August. It feels very like Kent, late summer, the sound of that motorbike, when it gets dark.

So, in *Sound Mirrors*, the sound is the most important part, while the images are more illustrative in a way.

The sound is the most important part, because that is what the mirrors were constructed for. But there is another thing to it. I am very interested in things that have lost their function, that were built in a visionary way, built as an idea and then they never really successfully functioned in society and were just neglected. That is what they are too, remnants of somebody's inspiration, and I like that. I like these strange monoliths that sit in this no place. They do illustrate the sound, that's true, but it's more than that, because they are very beautiful structures. The work was actually a commission for the National Theatre on the South Bank in London. They have this project that is called "Fourth Wall", which is basically the exterior wall of the backdrop of the National Theatre, a huge concrete wall. They were commissioning works to be projected there. I thought about *Sound Mirrors* in relation to that, which is very brutalist architecture, and there's a similarity between the structures somehow.

You have shown other films outside of the exhibition space, but in general you still choose to show your work there. Why?

Even *Banewl*, which is a 63-minute film, did not work in a cinema. The scale was too big and there was too much light, because cinemas are never dark enough places actually. It has to do with the audience as well. It has come as a progression. I actually did painting at art school. I always used to work in series, so I organically went on to film. And it is interesting that when I went to the Sundance Screenwriters Lab, I took with me *The Martyrdom of St Agatha (in several parts)*, which is a very narrative film and has a very tight narrative structure. I also took with me *Disappearance at Sea*, which is much more related to sculpture. *The Martyrdom of St Agatha (in several parts)* had a terrible time in England with the art press. The art people for some reason never liked it. However, the people at the Sundance Institute, which is "cinema film", loved *The Martyrdom of St Agatha (in several parts)*, but did not get *Disappearance at Sea* at all. It has so much to do with audience and it has so much to do with the nature of narrative. My films are related to space and sculpture. *Disappearance at Sea* particularly is related to the relationship between the projector and the screen and the bulbs; the projecting light, both in the image and in the space. The screens are a very specific size. It is all very controlled. In cinemas you do not have that control and I need that control for my films, because they are more jewel-like. It is very interesting, they do not work in cinemas, they are not made for cinemas, that structure does not work.

Another reason to show your films in exhibition galleries is that you can show several of them simultaneously in adjacent spaces, combined with other media. What strikes me is that on many levels there are links between the works, but that these links sometimes also shift. Some more recent films are linking perfectly to earlier films, that formerly linked with others. So the combination of works also builds the levels at which we can look at them.

What strikes me while organising this exhibition at MACBA and the one at Tate Britain in London, is that there are so many connections across time, I mean even discovering how much *A Bag of Air* has got to do with *Totality* is quite interesting.

In what sense?

Well, they both are about the sky. It never crossed my mind until I started to put them together. It is a curatorial thing; it is not a major conceptual thing. There are similarities, even if they were made five years apart. *Delft Hydraulics* suddenly works very well with *The Structure of Ice*, because they both relate to "pseudo-science".

Filming *Delft Hydraulics*, De Voorst, The Netherlands, 1996. (Photo: Esther Boender)

In *Banewl* we see the total eclipse of the sun of 1999, going from light to dark and back to light again, which we can mainly see through the reaction of the farm animals, for instance. How did you come to choose and film this subject, this very normal, or maybe even old-fashioned scenery, this dairy farm?

That had so much to do with the day, because that was not the film I intended to make, and that is often what happens, actually.

Because it was cloudy.

Yes. What happened is that I went down way in advance because there was obviously an eclipse fever in England. We wanted to find a south-facing place where you could see the sea in relation to the land. Also, it had to have trees, as I wanted to do detail work with the pinhole effect through trees. So it was quite a specific kind of thing. We found this dairy farm and this farmer who

Filming *Banewl*, Burnewhall Farm, St Buryan, Cornwall, 1999. (Photo: Richard Torchia)

83

was going to give it up by the end of August, and the eclipse was August 11. They were supposed to go on holiday for that week but they had not decided what to do with their farm,
knowing that this eclipse was going on. So it was perfect synchronicity. What happened in
effect is that the family went on holiday, but the farmer had to stay because they were sell-
ing up. For this reason we could rent the whole farm. I was interested in the real-time element of the eclipse, which is actually two hours and forty minutes. My ambition was to make
a real-time film of the eclipse, which would have really pushed tolerance, but I was very
keen on the fact that actual totality is only in the centre point, and is only one tiny fraction
of the entire event. I actually had enough film and it was an incredibly choreographed thing.
With film, it is all on ten minute reels, there had to be film in at least one camera at a time
so that I could cut it together in real time. That was how the film was actually made,
bearing that in mind. There were a lot of people involved in this production. Everybody knew
when to start their cameras because we knew when totality was, we could be really precise.
The day before we had a dummy run with four cameras, loaders and runners taking the films
back to the loaders etc. It was extraordinary. I have never been in charge of such a big event.
It was a beautiful cloudless day. The next morning it was raining and totally overcast. I
really insisted while everybody said: "Should we not film?" I said: "No, no, no, we film, we
film regardless of the circumstances, we film 'real-time', we film." We also had a camera
looking at the sun and a special sort of satellite control which was moving so the sun was
always in the centre of the frame. It was a real business. My cameraman kept on ringing
me up on this walkie-talkie, saying: "You cannot see anything, it is all grey." And I said:
"No, John, you've got to film, you've got to film." In the end I had nine hours of footage, a
lot of it really grey. In the end I made it into a 63-minute film which is under half of the
length of the eclipse. But it is totally chronological, it is chronologically correct. The whole
film, which is very important actually, is happening during the eclipse. Even when the farmer
takes the cows down to the field, the eclipse is going on: it's just you cannot see it. It is all
happening during a cosmic event.

The cows were not taken out at six in the morning or so?
Oh yes, we asked him to hold the cows for an hour or so after milking, which he did do for us.

So you had an idea of what you wanted to do, which was impossible because of the circumstances. In this case you had to work from the footage, away from your original idea.
With me, everything is in the process of editing. It really is the essential part of my films. It
has been like that with all of them. With *Teignmouth Electron* and *Banewl*, it is the only time

I have not actually cut my own sound on magnetic tape to go with the film. I have actually post-produced the sound. With *Banewl* it was a phenomenal feat for sound and there was no way I could do that without going to a post-production place. In *Banewl*, and people will be heartbroken to find this out, even the cows are foley. With *Teignmouth Electron* I really needed an aeroplane, so I just decided to go and do it with Steve and his post-production place. Usually, I always have edited the sound with the image and that has been a very important part of the whole thing as well. I love working with sound.

You mentioned *Foley Artist* before, which was quite an analytical work about sound in cinema. If you look at it now and compare it to later films with more complex, layered sound constructs, and to your sound works, how do you see the work?

Well, *Foley Artist* was designed without an image. But as soon as I saw the foley artists in action I had to film them. It is a very eccentric profession, the banging and clashing of things. I love the way sound is so constructed in cinema and playing with that, playing with the gap between sound and image. The best filmmakers for me are the ones that do that.

Filming *Foley Artist*, Sheperton Studios, 1996. (Photo: Stephen White)

The trouble with Hollywood is, of course, that it is all too sewn up. It does not allow for any imaginative space. *Foley Artist* was a very explanatory piece, it explained a lot to me, strangely. When I look at it, it fills me with great nostalgia and a kind of happiness because it reminds me of a certain time and it makes me feel warm towards cinema, real cinema, because that was what it was all about. It is a really old job. Obviously the two foley artists I used were deliberately pretty old.

Are the days of the foley artist almost over?

They were actually. But ironically, with digital sound they need them more now than ever.

How come?

Because obviously most sound in film is sound effects coming from compact discs. If people realised how much comes from compact discs! When a sound editor listens to any Hollywood film he recognises exactly which sound effect comes from which compact disc. But the one thing they still cannot do is generic footsteps, because everyone is different. And a generic putting down of a glass, stuff like that. You really do need a foley, you need someone to do it specifically to the film. So it is actually getting bigger, rather than less, which is nice to know.

Foley artists, through their work for cinema, determine how we think something sounds in real life, while digital Hollywood sounds do not sound like the "real thing" anymore. At the same time they use foleys as well.

Sound has become more important and ironically also because of the Dolby system, whereas it just used to be second place within cinema. What I really like about the whole foley thing is that, as you were saying, there are all these cinema tricks for producing sound that become how we imagine we hear footsteps. You don't hear footsteps like you do in cinema, but it actually has infiltrated into real life. How we imagine we hear footsteps has entirely derived from cinema. It comes back on itself. It has gone through cinema and out again. If you look at a film without foley, you just think that someone has turned the sound down. You do not hear people going clonk clonk clonk. We imagine that that is what we do hear, even in real life.

You did some other sound works, the first one being *Trying to Find the Spiral Jetty*. How did that come about?

I was at the Sundance Screenwriters Lab, and just because I was in Utah and someone told me that the *Spiral Jetty* had risen again I decided that I wanted to go find it. At that time, because I was in this real cinema screenwriting place, it felt very much like finding an icon from my former life, from my art school world, rather than the cinema world. Although I loved it, I was quite thoroughly out of context there. I went off to find the *Spiral Jetty* with a guy from the Screenwriters Lab who did not know what he was looking for. I had no intention to make an artwork; I just happened to have my DAT recorder with me. The journey became more and more convoluted and peculiar and we got further and further away from civilisation, following these directions from the Utah Arts Council. They were directions from 1 to 12 and at point 10, I do not know why, I just turned my DAT on, just to record our conversation. I do not know why in particular I did that. And then we had this sort of accident in which the car got stuck on a rock and then we could not find the damn thing. There was another kind of jetty, I still do not know if that was it or not, the beginning of it. It could have been an oil-drilling jetty. I had not even been so fanatic about Smithson either, but when I got back to New York, I bought his collected writings. On the site I had collected all this salined tumble-weed. And I found that in his book there were all these photographs of the same stuff. It was that thing about recognition. I got very excited about it and I started to read about the *Spiral Jetty* and how it – for him – was about all sorts of things, the primeval world, the sun, and about film as well. And when I got back to England, I had a show in September. I just decided – it was a kind of interesting relation to the Screenwriters Lab I had been to – that I was going to try to fabricate points 1 to 10 with the guy I went out there with, who lived in Los Angeles. I asked him to try and remember our conversation and I had to try and remember our conversation as well. So I was in King's Cross in London, recording under my duvet because of the traffic noise. I tried to record "Oh, we turn right here" etc., but I was painfully self-conscious that it was fake. I sent it to him and he did much better than me and he sent it back to me. Actually, I scripted what he had said and I gave my answers and then I edited it all together with sound effects, including my car driving down a dirt track in Oxford and cattlegrids and all sorts of stuff that I recorded. So I made it into a fiction. And at a point the real soundtrack comes in. So it's half fake and half real, which I always like when I describe it because it reminds me of Crowhurst, when my false journey meets my real journey, it was a bit the same for him, that moment.

You did another Smithson-based work. Did you get taken by his work after reading his writings?

It is kind of strange. I ended up in Ohio on a month's residency at the Wexner Art Center and without an idea. There is nothing more paralysing than having a residency without an

SPIRAL JETTY

Detailed directions:

1. Go to the Golden Spike National Historic Site (GSNHS), 30
miles west of Brigham City, Utah. The Spiral Jetty is 15.5
dirt-road miles southwest of the GSNHS.

To get there (from Salt Lake City) take I-80 north
approximately 65 miles to the Corinne exit, just west of
Brigham City, Utah. Exit and proceed 2.5 miles west, on
State Highway 83, to Corinne. Proceed through Corinne,
and drive another 17.7 miles west, still on highway 83,
to Lampo Junction. Turn west off highway 83 at Lampo,
and drive 7.7 miles up the east side of Promontory Pass
to the GSNHS.

2. From the Visitor Center at the GSNHS, drive 5.6 miles west
on the main dirt road running west from the Center. Remember
to take the county dirt road...not the railroad grade.

3. Five point six miles will bring you to an intersection.
From this vantage you can see the lake. And looking
southwest, you can see the low foot hills that make up Rozel
Point, 9.9 miles distant.

4. At this intersection the road forks: One road continues
west and the other goes south. Take the south fork. Both
forks are Box Elder County Class D (maintained) roads.

5. Immediately you cross a cattle guard. Call this cattle
guard #1. Including this one, you will cross four cattle
guards before you reach Rozel Point and the Spiral Jetty.

6. Drive 1.3 miles south. Here you will see a corral on the
west side of the road. Here too, the road again forks. One
fork continues south along the Promontory Mountains. This
road leads to a locked gate. The other fork goes southwest
toward the bottom of the valley and Rozel Point. Turn onto
the southwest fork, just north of the corral. This is also a
Box Elder County Class D road.

7. After you turn southwest, you will go 1.7 miles to cattle
guard #2. Here, besides the cattle guard, you will find a
fence but no gate.

8. Continue southeast 1.2 miles to cattle guard #3, a fence,
a gate, and a sign on the gate which reads, "Promontory
Ranch."

9. Another .50 miles will bring you to a fence but no cattle
guard and no gate.

10.   Continue 2.3 miles south/southwest to a combination

fence, cattle guard #4, iron-pipe gate...and a sign declaring
the property behind the fence to be that of the Rafter S
Ranch. Here too, is a "No Trespassing" sign.

11.   If you choose to continue south for another 2.3 miles,
and around the east side of Rozel Point, you will see the
Lake and a jetty (not the Spiral Jetty) left by oil drilling
exploration in the 1950's. As you approach the Lake, you will
see an abandoned, pink and white trailer (mostly white), an
old army amphibious landing craft, an old Dodge truck...and
other assorted trash.

The trailer is the key to finding the road to the Spiral
Jetty. As you drive slowly past the trailer, turn immediately
to the west, passing on the south side of the Dodge, and onto
a two-track trail that contours above the oil-drilling debris
below. This is not much of a road! In fact, at first glance
it might not look to be a road at all. Go slow! The road is
narrow; brush might scratch your vehicle, and the rocks, if
not properly negotiated, could high center your vehicle.

12.   Drive .6 miles west/northwest around Rozel Point and look
toward the Lake. The Spiral Jetty should be in sight.

Maps of the area:
        BLM 1:100,000 Surface Management maps - Available at the
        BLM's State Office Public Room, 324 South State Street,
        Salt Lake City, Utah 84111 phone: (801) 539-4001
                (1)   Tremonton
                (2)   Promontory

        U.S. Geological Survey, 7.5 minute series - Available at
        the U.S.G.S., Federal Building, 125 South State Street,
        Salt Lake City, Utah 84111 phone: (801) 524-5652
                (1)   Golden Spike Monument Quadrangle
                (2)   Rozel Quadrangle
                (3)   Rozel Point Quadrangle

For Additional Information:

        Bureau Of Land Management
        Salt Lake District
        2370 South 2300 West
        Salt Lake City, Utah 84119
        phone: (801) 977-4300

        Golden Spike National Historic Site
        P. O. Box 897
        Brigham City, Utah 84302
        phone: (801) 471-2209

Rozel Point, Great Salt Lake, Utah, 1997 (slide projection)

idea. The only thing I had and knew about in Ohio was that the *Partially Buried Woodshed* was in Kent State. I persuaded the people who were with me at the media place of the Wexner Art Center to come with me on a day trip. We recorded it on video. It was a very video experience, a real-time campus hideousness. So we did make a video which is all about the fact that the *Partially Buried Woodshed* is not where it is supposed to be, I am sure it is under the carpark. I was so lucky being at the Wexner, because they had been given a gift of some super 8 footage, taken by students who helped Smithson do the *Partially Buried Woodshed.* So I was allowed to use this footage which meant that we actually had something to compare it to. We drew maps about where we thought it was in relation to the black-and-white footage. We realised that where they have a sort of little lump in the campus map is not where you see the shed is, on the super 8 films. There were three buildings, and it is not possible that it could be where the campus now says it is. So again I really did not find it. The video portrays how kind of corporate and campus-like that whole situation has become, as opposed to how radical a thing it was in 1970. Especially with the Kent State uprising. It is really buried now in a particular way.

Did you also want to demonstrate that there is a difference between film and video, since most of your other work is film?

Yes, totally. This is a day trip, real-time kind of experience. In no way can it be a vehicle for an allegorical time or historical time or anything like that. Although I did intercut some of the students' super 8 film. That sounds a bit funny, because I never usually use anyone else's material and I would never normally put film onto video. I use film in a very different way to video.

Vito Acconci once said: "Film is landscape and silence, while video is close-up and sound."

I agree with that. It is a beautiful thing to have said. Even though most of my films do have sound, they are very much about silence. We talked about that in relation to dark rooms and events. Video has this relationship to television, the relation between the television set and the video monitor is very strong. They could be in a fairly bright room as well.

For you, one reason to work in film is that it is a medium of time. While editing, you literally cut out pieces of time with which you construct your work. It is very physical. Could you elaborate more on the importance of time in your work?

I do not know how to say it too deliberately, but I have a certain pace to my films and it is really intuitive in terms of cutting shots. As an artist making films I am quite formal. I do not tend to use pans or zooms. I like the static shot that allows for things to happen in the frame, and I think that is why the time thing is so important. It is very difficult to say I am interested in time, it is like saying: "I am interested in the sea." It is just allowing the space and time for whatever to happen, and that comes very much from the nature of film, definitely. In that sense the whole process is very important. It is not just cutting out pieces of time, but the way you cut a film has totally to do with chronology, it is linear in a sense. You can never jump to the bit you want to work on. You have to watch the whole film again, even if you fast-forward it or rewind it. There is the constant ritual of time. It is a very strong part of the process; in fact, extremely strong in the process. And all the other things that come through, like the whole idea of editing in order to make time look seamless. That is interesting because that has very much to do with film. With film you have to edit out of necessity whereas with video you edit out of a sort of luxury. With film you have your magazine of 400 feet, which is ten minutes and then it stops. Then you have to go somewhere else or you jump cut. Or you have 2.5-minute magazines, like I normally use. I tend to hold the frame until my film runs out, so I am very extravagant at that point. Everything else is quite frugal in my process except for the fact that I shoot quite a lot of film.

When you look at the number of shots in *Bubble House*, for instance, which is seven minutes, the one through the window is very long.

It is a whole magazine of 2.5 minutes.

As I mentioned before, I think that in your films the shots are becoming more static and
longer. That has to do with what you say about allowing things to happen within static shots.
It seems that your films are getting slower in a way.

They get slower with these static shots, because you are not distracted by the movement of
the camera. You are actually looking within the frame. It does allow for a different sort of
time realisation. I do not know why that attracts me. There is nothing deliberate about it,
it is just how I started to make the films.

Does it also have to do with slowing down the speed at which we are used to encountering
images nowadays, especially with media and computer-based works? Your films are supposed to be seen from the beginning to the end, as there always is a beginning and an end
as well as an event around which the film evolves.

I know. I do not think I am slowing down time, but I think I am demanding people's time. With
Banewl I really wanted to push it to the very limits of boredom. Or waiting. That piece is about
waiting. It is waiting for a cosmic event. I wanted to get that across. And I wanted to get
across the anticlimax as well, and the return to a normal sun as well. That whole thing was
about symmetry. It is amazing how the quality of the nature of time changed after the eclipse.
The anticipation sped it up in a way. Whereas the anticlimax, waiting for it to be over, became
something else. A sort of very strange time when life was not normal, quite, but had the ap-
parent feeling of it. I extended the second half of the film to put that across. That sort of
change, that shifting time quality, that counting down, because of the getting darker and darker. Had it been an incredibly clear sky, I would have been able to make it the way I planned.
I wanted to make a real film. There had never been an official document of the total eclipse.
So I wanted to do it for that reason also. Because everybody does the first half, but not the
second, because it is almost unbearable. You want to go and put your head under a blanket
after the totality. But you have to sit through the other half, the symmetry. So when it was
cloudy, in a way it delivered me from that. It shifted everything. It became about the ground
and the place, as well as the sky, but not as much about the sky as I had imagined. And not as
much about the cosmic phenomena. It became about the reflections of the clouds on the ground,
what was happening below. The relation of this strange event, this darkening, to the cows
and so on. And it became much more about the animals and their reaction to it.

But you still made a film about the sky, *Totality*. Why did you decide to make a film about the sky while it was so cloudy?

Totality is totally about the sky and it is a very abstract work. This was the footage that was taken at the same time as *Banewl*, obviously. It was the footage from the camera that was focused on the sun which magnified it thirty times its normal size. The motion-tracking device meant the sun was always in the middle of the frame. It becomes just about the shift of tone. You lose track that it is the sky until at the very end you notice the movement of a cloud and then a bird flies across the frame.

So it is more like a natural fade out and fade in?

I always think it is more like colour field painting. It is like different shades and tones. It is very abstract. It is eleven minutes long. It is mute as well. It is a very experimental work, different from my usual.

In relation to your work you mentioned sculpture before, and now colour field painting. Do your films relate more to art than to cinema?

Definitely. In this new film I am making, *Fernsehturm*, there is a moment when it looks like an Edward Hopper painting. Really, so like an Edward Hopper painting. It is very referential to painting. And a lot of my films have that reference in them somehow. Not that I seek it out.

But it is just there.

It is just there. Like with *Banewl* everybody goes on about Constable. It is subliminal of course, and I am an English pastoral artist. I am sure that the influence is all there. I got an e-mail from Marian Goodman Gallery asking: "Was she thinking of Constable?" The answer is: "No, I was not". But I was thinking about the English landscape, so maybe the two have become inseparable now.

Another thing in relation to your films and the time element are these drawings on blackboards. They are not storyboards in the sense that they are used for a film that you are going to make, but autonomous works. You call them storyboards, or not?

I call them dysfunctional storyboards. They are non-chronological. They do not work in any way as storyboards, they could not function as storyboards. They also have the same quality as post-production stills as well. They are a mixture of the two.

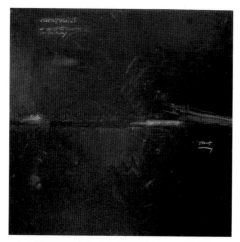

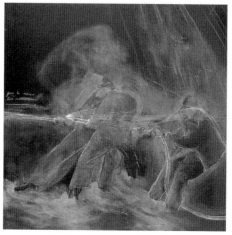

94

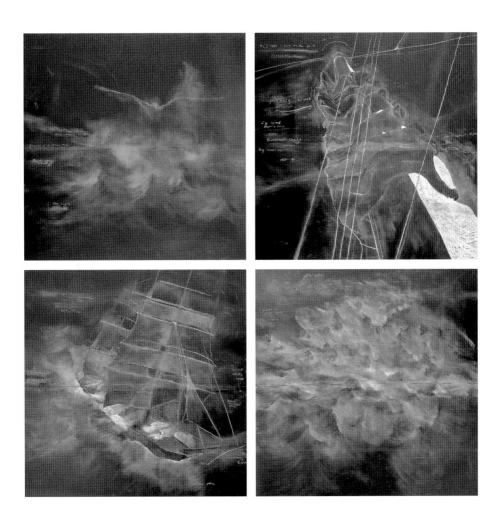

The Roaring Forties: Seven Boards in Seven Days, 1997

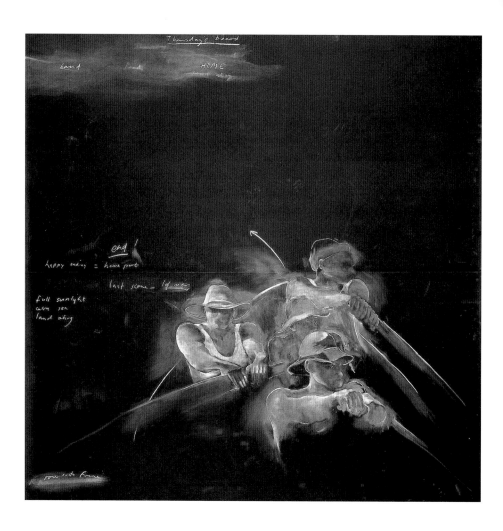

96

But there is always an action, a passage of time going on within each blackboard. They are not still images, but rather in-between images.

They have a very hybrid quality. They do not function in the normal world in any way really.

Are you still doing them?

I am trying to do a forest. I have been trying to leave the sea. But the problem with that is that the sea is so intricately connected to them. Because of the flux, the drawing and the erasure, the whole process is so like the nature and the movement of the sea. That is not just a flabby analogy at all. It is actually how they are constructed. It is very difficult to draw something that is static, that does not have that flux. So I do not know if I will be able to do them in any other way, other than the sea.

You do works with strips of 16 mm magnetic tape. How do they function in relation to your other works?

The idea was born from the soundtrack of *A Bag of Air*, which in the end I never made into a magnetic piece. It was the sounds of all the different types of air: lower-air, mid-air and upper-air, all these recordings from going up in a hot air balloon. But I never made it because they do not have definitive cut-off points. And I started to think about things that did. Like a bird's cry, a seagull's cry. I made a seagull as a present for someone and that started off the whole thing. They are the transcriptions of sound through time. It is like making time concrete. Making it a physical thing that you look at.

Seagull (Magnetic), 1997

You have a clover collection. How did this collection enter your art?

I showed it in 1995. I am very interested in collections anyway and this is my collection of four-leaf clovers and five-, six- and one seven-leaf clover. I started it when I was eight. It became art in a very sort of strange way. A bit personal. A friend of mine died and I could not go to his funeral because it was in Ireland, but I went down to Cornwall to throw some flowers in the sea for him. On my way I found this huge supply of four-leaf clovers. And I found this seven-leaf clover. I knew it was a sort of blessing in a way. I decided then I would like to show them in my exhibition at the Frith Street Gallery in London. Because in a way they are invested with hope and charms, the whole thing about luck. It is a very strange relationship I have with them, it is the same relationship I have with coincidence. In this way I am very superstitious and Catholic. I think if I stop being able to find them, my luck will end or something. It is like having coincidences. If I stop having them it is all over. I have a real facility to find four-leaf clovers. It is very strange. I have already found some here in the Grünewald, here in Berlin.

But they also relate to *A Bag of Air, The Structure of Ice* and *Gellért?*

The healing theme. Well, I made this little book that went with the clover collection which is about the fact that a cow is "a capable chemist". They select clover because it is so alkaline. It is a good anti-acid thing. It is good against this disease they have, the sore teets, mastitis, and people think this disease is very close to arthritis. So there was a connection between the clover and arthritis in an extremely weird way, which I got from this book called *Arthritis and Folklore*. It is all connected in a way.

Do these works also have to do with your position as an artist? I think someone wrote about *A Bag of Air* as being about artistic production, transforming invaluable substances into something valuable.

Well, the example of the artist as an alchemist is very often used and that piece is a lot about alchemy. To some extent that is true. Not that that was going on in my head.

But that is what happens when you put it in the real world.

Yes. I was interested in the whole thing about the Rosicrucians catching dew. This story is another example of charm, of things going wrong in order to go right. I wanted to catch clouds in a hot air balloon. However, hot air balloons do not go up if there is any sign of cloud, so I tried to find a place famous for

Palais Jacques Coeur, Bourges 1995
(Photo: Jean Frémiot)

morning mist. Yet that morning, there was no mist and I actually had to catch clear air, which at the time was very disappointing. Then I came back and started my research into alchemy and saw that alchemy had very much to do with the four ethers that the Rosicrucians used to catch in the form of dew going up and rain coming down. And I looked up "ether" and it said: "clear sky, upper air". Which is unbelievable. It was like such a gift. It suddenly all made sense that I was there collecting cloudless air. And then there was the philosopher's stone and all the mystery ingredients in alchemy. I thought it was an "R" as the French say it, "air", because there was a missing "R" in this alchemical palace in Bourges, which is all very complicated but it made perfect sense to me. Actually air is the secret food of life. Then I found out that what the alchemists did produce was *phlogiston*, before they understood pure oxygen. Which is air, it is all about air. And then the first alchemist managed to go under the Thames with *phlogiston* in effectively the first submarine, and his alchemy was air. People think *A Bag of Air* is a very "bio" film, very green: going over the smog to catch clean air.

Though of course it is beyond that.

Yes, totally. But it has a lot of hope in it, doesn't it?

Isn't there hope in most of your work?

People think there is a lot of loss in my work.

In which sense?

Things are disappearing, *Disappearance at Sea*, the loss of Crowhurst and the loss of function of these buildings. Disintegration and entropy.

The "Hope Suitcase", 2000. (Photo: Tacita Dean)

Sometimes the word nostalgia comes up in relation to your work, but I think that you transform these things lost and forgotten and give them new meaning by using them to communicate a message of hope.

Maybe. I had this suitcase that I used to run away with when I was a child. It was called the "Hope Suitcase". It has "hope" written on it in white, very beautifully painted.

Did you paint it yourself?

No, my mother bought it from a convent in Ramsgate.

A suitcase with "hope" written on it?

It was obviously from a nun who was called Hope. Sister Hope. It is really beautiful, because it is hand painted, "hope". I always made it my suitcase when I was little. It is here now, I am looking at it. It has all my tax in it now, which is not very good for it. But it is interesting, hope/loss.

How important is writing for you? In this book are collected all the texts related to your work. You call them *asides*, a term used in Shakespearean theatre. One does not need to read the texts to look at the work. They do not explain the work but are separate entities.

They are separate entities and they sit side by side with the work. Theodora Vischer put it so beautifully in her afterword for the publication of the Museum für Gegenwartskunst in Basel: "Text and films, or other works, use different methods to circle around the same theme. Dean has called this collection of stories an *aside*. 'An aside' is a term taken from Shakespearean theatre, and denotes something which an actor speaks directly to the audience, without affecting the action on the stage." Which I think is great. So they do sit parallel to the works and actually I want to give them a sort of legitimacy, so that it is something else, not just a text but another part of the work.

However, they are not with the works in the space. They are always published in a book, which already gives them a different status. But you always write texts, for all works?

Some are the spoken narratives from the films. Usually the others come from writing something after the work is finished, and usually when they are to be published in some form.

You got this commission for the Millennium Dome, for which you recorded sound around the world?

Well, the Millennium Dome was a god-awful place, even then. They wanted some artists to do something in the scrubland around it. Not inside it, but outside it. The only thing that caught my interest even remotely was this ventilation shaft. A French-looking Victorian mushroom-shaped building with eight sides and an overhanging roof. Quite a nice building. What the shaft does is to suck

Recording in the bus shelter, Naselesele, Fiji, 2000.
(Photo: Mathew Hale)

air down into the Blackwall Tunnel every time the carbon dioxide levels get too high. It has a very loud sound when they suck the air in. It starts screaming for at least an hour each day. The vent was made of raw cement. My request was to keep it exactly as it was and of course they promptly painted it. Also the Meridian Line went right through it and they promptly moved that as well. As the vent was originally on the Meridian Line, which is longitude 0 degrees in Greenwich, and because it had eight sides, I decided to divide the world into eight longitudes, and where the longitude line cut through land and sea at a port, I would go to that place and record 24 hours of ambient sound between midday Friday and Saturday because that was the Millennium transition: *Friday/Saturday*, which is what I called the piece. They would all run totally within their own time, so it was all about time zones and sound, 45 degrees around the world. So 45 degrees east of Greenwich is Aden in Yemen which is exactly on the longitude line, and then Dhaka in Bangladesh is 90 degrees east and Akashi in Japan, 135 degrees east and then Fiji, of course, is 180 degrees. 135 degrees west is Alaska and then New Orleans is 90 degrees west and then Ubatuba, which is a port in Brazil, is 45 degrees west, and Greenwhich obviously is zero. Because I had such a limited amount of time I sent friends to three of these places and I went to the other five. We recorded 24 hours of sound on each location from midday Friday to midday Saturday, and at the Millennium Dome they play simultaneously so you can actually walk around at midnight and hear midday in Fiji. Sound is so descriptive. It is incredibly descriptive. You can actually go there and everybody is awake. Potentially it could have been quite a nice thing but it was completely ruined by the Millennium Dome.

So they were all playing the actual times of their own time zone simultaneously?

Yes. It was running for 24 hours a day, 365 days a year. But the sad thing is that people only hear it from 10 am to 5 pm because of the opening hours. So then I took all the sounds out in fact and turned it into *Jukebox*, so you could chose where you wanted to be around the world.

Why a machine like a jukebox?

This is interesting because I could have done it all digitally. The whole installation in the Dome is digital, all computers. But I really

Friday/Saturday, Millenium Dome, London, 2000.
(Photo: Tacita Dean)

wanted to go back to a way in which people would be able to physically select something. So I made 192 compact discs, which of course no jukebox would play. Therefore I had to build my own. It is a completely weird prototype, it is a monster really. A really strange thing. And you choose your location and an hour and press play and it plays in the space. It is a pretty weird thing. It is strange because its roots came from elsewhere. In a way it is a very odd piece of work, because the places are no longer specific to the sides of the ventilation shaft. Its provenance is very weird, you do not get it. Why Ubatuba, why Yemen?

You can figure it out from the knobs on the machine with which you can choose where to go. Yes, they have got the places and longitude degrees on them. So you can figure it out.

What interests me is that a jukebox is for selecting what you want to hear, but this is all real recordings, real sound at real time. You do not know what you are going to get. It is like travelling through time and space, like a time machine.

It is a bit like a time machine. It is funny how these things happen. In a way it was being created like that, in the way we were designing it very specifically. It had to look like a cross between a Star Trek prop and something contemporary. It was a strange hybrid thing. But I did not want it to look too sci-fi. I wanted it to refer to a jukebox. But obviously it is not, it is something different. But it is in between the bridge of a ship and the bridge of a starship. It is interesting in relation to time travel. It is all about times and places that you can go to at any chosen moment.

In relation to this work, you have made photographs on each location. In this way they represent the location. What is the function of photography in relation to works like *Bubble House* and *Teignmouth Electron*, for which you did both film and photos?

For *Teignmouth Electron* I took these photographs for the book. The black-and-white aerial photograph has this haunting quality which could relate to all sorts of other things other than just Crowhurst, like Smithson, as you said. One of them I call "J. G. Ballard". It is the one in the undergrowth, which I think

Juke Box 2, 2000. Installation at the Museum für Gegenwartskunst, Basel, 2000. (Photo: Martin Bühler)

is such a strange image surrounded by trees, because you get no sense of the sea there. It is just greenery and this boat. The other one is a very sort of mournful photograph, with the storm coming, this heavy cloud in the background. They are such compelling images that I think they are strong enough to survive alongside the film. And the ones for *Bubble House* in a way came first as well. They are not stills from the film at all. They are taken beside the film. I first took the photographs and then the film, like with *Teignmouth Electron*.

How do you choose on the format and presentation of your films, like the anamorphic format and the size of the image?

When I first chose anamorphic, it was for *Disappearance at Sea* because I very much wanted the sense of the light of the lighthouse travelling through the frame. That is why I wanted an extended frame. That was one reason. The second reason was that it was to be shown in a lighthouse in Berwick, which was only six feet in diameter, which is very small. I wanted the image to sort of curl around inside the interior. So I investigated into a sort of Cinemascope format for 16 mm, which is anamorphic. It is quite rare. There is only one guy doing these lenses. It worked very well for that film, this format. So I used it for *Disappearance at Sea II*, which was filmed at the same time. And then when it came to the eclipse film, *Banewl*, I thought it would be a perfect format for the eclipse, because of the whole expanse of landscape and skyscape. What I imagined was going to happen was the shadow rushing through the landscape towards you. And again I have chosen it for the new film, *Fernsehturm*, because of the format of the building. It is a round tower with a revolving restaurant. I am filming in the interior, filming the windows, which are almost slanting outwards. So you also need an extended frame for the movement of the chairs and the tables through the frame. Some films call for an extended frame and others do not.

And this format resembles the screen we know from the cinema.

No, that is widescreen, Cinemascope is wider still than widescreen.

But the format looks like it, it is obviously different from normal 16 mm or TV and video size. Do you know any other filmmakers or artists that were already working with this format?

There are a few 16 mm prints that are like domestic versions of 35 mm prints that are on anamorphic. That is why it is mostly used, I think. The guy who sells and rents these lenses sometimes does not have them, which means that people are using them in some form. But I think they are only using them as part of a process to get somewhere else. I have never seen a finished product of 16 mm film in this format and definitely not in the art world. This format of 1 to 2.55, this anamorphic lens, disperses the light twice as far. They have to be shown quite small so that they have a certain intensity. That is why the projection of *Banewl* did not work on a cinema scale. But also because it was beyond life-size. Especially with this film. The cows were enormous, which did not function. These are not films for cinemas, they are films for exhibition galleries. They were made that way. They do not have many of the conventions of cinema. That is why I have to make a space especially for them. And each one differs slightly. For *Banewl* it is a 10-foot screen, suspended on the wall. And the screen is cut to the anamorphic lens. So it is that specific. Every time I have a presentation people have to cut the screen to the lens, because every anamorphic lens is slightly different. I have it slightly away from the wall, so that the shadow caused by the screen makes it a more three-dimensional image. *Delft Hydraulics* I show that waist height and quite small. This is quite intuitive, but it is obvious why in a way. It is a very sexy film. And then the film *Sound Mirrors* is either front or backprojected, filling the whole wall more like a bunker. The decision of black and white and colour is sometimes a practical decision. I brought black-and-white stock to shoot *Gellért* in Budapest. But when I was there the colours were so extreme that I had to get colour stock sent over. The black-and-white stock was left over and I used it for *Sound Mirrors* but I knew black and white would work better projected at that scale and with all that ambient light. For *Delft Hydraulics,* when we went there I thought it would have been beautiful in colour. It is not always a clear decision.

Filming *Sound Mirrors* in b/w was not a deliberate choice because of the greyness of the concrete structures?

That is what I mean, which is really strange, and what I do not want to deny is that accidents are very important to peoples' art making. I think a lot of people underestimate that. I say accidents, which is the extreme end of it, but the fact is that you have it there and use it. It may be intuitive or whatever. What is really weird with my new film, *Fernsehturm,* is that it just looks like it is surrounded by sea. It really strongly looks like the prow

The Fernsehturm, Berlin, 2000.
(Photo: Tacita Dean, Mathew Hale)

of a boat moving through the sea. It is unbelievable. I do not know how I have managed to make a film about the sea in the middle of Berlin, but I have. You see the horizon and Berlin becomes this sort of grey blue, the white flecks of buildings just become white horses.

Would you not prefer to call it "chance", rather than "accident"?

Sometimes things do go wrong; like for *Banewl*, it being cloudy when I wanted to film the total eclipse.

But what about when you travel a long way, for instance when you went to the Cayman Islands to film Crowhurst's boat, did you know what you were going to find and did you have a clear idea of what you wanted to do when you decided to go there?

The thing is I went to photograph it and not to film it. Because I was taking photographs for my book. And then the Maritime Museum got on board and gave me a large-format camera and film in order to get it documented for them also. So I have ten photographs that are in their archive. I took a 16 mm camera just for myself. I took ten rolls of film, which is not very much. Each roll is 2.5 minutes. But I was documenting this boat and then we drove along the road and found the "Bubble House". So I had to share the footage, which was already a very small amount, between both *Bubble House* and *Teignmouth Electron*. That is why they are cut quite tightly, I did not have a lot to choose from. I was very blessed for *Bubble House*, because of the storm coming in.

So this was another thing that just came by chance. Otherwise you would have documented it like the *Teignmouth Electron* and then work from there.

Yes. In fact it happened because of the storm. In the end I would never had been able to make a film out of it if it was not for that shot through the window. I set the camera up filming in all innocence because it was a complete crisp blue horizon when I started. And literally a storm came in. It was quite extraordinary, completely transformative. I used that shot as the centrepoint for the whole film, because that was the event. There was no thunder in real life, but I had to build up the drama of it.

The "Bubble House" is another product of someone's vision, a house perfectly shaped for a windy and rainy climate. What was the story? Because it was left there unfinished, like a concrete skull.

The only information that we had access to came from the locals. There was a guy drinking beer there one night and he told us everyone called it "Bubble House". Then I found out from this guy who owned the *Teignmouth Electron* that it was owned by this Frenchman who was a property developer. There was big excitement when he built it. They had to blow up a balloon to cover it with cement. Then he got arrested for fraud and he is doing 35 years in Tampa Prison, I think, which is a horrific amount. So it is just completely left abandoned. At the bed and breakfast where we were staying was this guy from Cayman Brac and he really resented the fact that we were so interested in what he considered the two pieces of shame and neglect on his island. For me the island was absolutely unbearable, very claustrophobic, moneyed. And the only two places of interest to me were the Teignmouth Electron and the "Bubble house", obviously neglected in this well-preserved island. A very small island. You get a sense of that from the last shot of *Teignmouth Electron*, you see how small it is.

Teignmouth Electron, 1996 (film still)

How did the plane enter that film?

Well, the boat is right by the airport. What we tried to do the whole time was to film the plane taking off. And of course they take off from different directions for all sorts of reasons, so it became this crazy ritual trying to film the plane taking off. We would get up at all sorts of hours in the day just trying to film it. And at the end, I do not know if I saw it on the way over, but I knew exactly where the Teignmouth Electron was when we took off in the plane that we had been trying to film for a week. That was very lucky. We flew right over it.

To me it also feels a bit like a Robert Smithson echo, like him going up in a plane to film the *Spiral Jetty* or maybe the *Amarillo Ramp*, which became his fatal flight.

Maybe that is why I always put the aerial photograph of the Teignmouth Electron with my Smithson-related works. They somehow always go together. And I am sure it is that echo.

FILMOGRAPHY AND SOUND WORKS
BIOGRAPHY
BIBLIOGRAPHY

FILMOGRAPHY AND SOUND WORKS

The Story of Beard 1992
16 mm colour and black-and-white,
optical sound, voice-over, 8 minutes

CAST: Lucy Gunning, Robert Barr, Tacita Dean,
Philip Jones, Jo Lawrance, Christina McBride,
Jeanie O'Hare, Craig Peacock, Julia Thrift, Sara
Wicks · CAMERA: Tacita Dean, Christina McBride,
Julia Thrift · MUSIC: Philip Jones · OPTICAL PRINT-
ING: Nick Collins · SOUND TRANSFER: Steve Felton
STILLS: Jeanie O'Hare · NEG CUT: Trucut ·
PRINTED BY: Filmatic
Filmed on location in Prague, Kent and London ·
Supported by the Ray Finnis Charitable Trust and
The Slade School of Fine Art

The Martyrdom of St Agatha
(in several parts) 1994
16 mm colour, optical sound, voice-over,
14 minutes

CAST: Iris Athanasoula, Lucy Gunning,
Jo Lawrance, Christina McBride, Jeanie
O'Hare, Julia Thrift, Emma Tod · CAMERA: John
Adderley, Tacita Dean · CAMERA ASSISTANTS: Jamie
Cairney, Sara Wicks · SOUND ASSISTANTS: Tom
Wright, Steve C. Owen · MUSIC: Mavernie
Cunningham, Mark Pharoah, Warwick, Dominic
Weeks · SOUND TRANSFER: Steve Felton
BREAST CASTING: Rod Dickinson, Sara Wicks ·
TITLES: Stuart Crundwell · WITH THANKS: Katy
English, Tim Hodgkinson, Philip Jones, Lorraine
Miller, Craig Peacock, Martyn Ridgewell, Guy
Sherwin, Helen Underwood · EDITED AT: Four
Corners · DUBBED BY: Warwick Sound
NEG CUT: Triad · PRINTED BY: Rank Film
Laboratories

Filmed on location in Catania, Sicily, Wolver-
Hampton Iron Founders and London
Supported by the Arts Council of England

Girl Stowaway 1994
16 mm colour and black-and-white,
optical sound, 8 minutes

CAST: Monica Cariani, Aldo Anselmo, Nick Breese,
David Luck · CAMERA: Tacita Dean · SOUND TRANS-
FER: Steve Felton · WITH THANKS: John Adderley,
Marcus Davies, Martyn Ridgewell · EDITED AT:
Four Corners · DUBBED BY: Warwick Sound
NEG CUT: Triad · PRINTED BY: Rank Film
Laboratories
Filmed on location in Cornwall and Starehole
Bay, Devon
Supported by the London Arts Board

How to Put a Boat in a Bottle 1995
Video, colour with sound, 18 minutes

CAST: Jimmy Benny, Dorcas Benny, Tacita Dean,
Helen Thompson · CAMERA: Tacita Dean ·
WITH THANKS: David Luck, Gilles Martinez, Owen
Oppenheimer · EDITED AT: École Nationale des
Beaux-Arts de Bourges
Filmed on location in St Ives, Cornwall

A Bag of Air 1995
16 mm black-and-white, optical sound, voice-over,
3 minutes

CAST: Anthony Busi · HOT AIR BALLOON: Bruno
Guérin, Patrick Poussardin · CAMERA: Tacita Dean
SOUND TRANSFER: Steve Felton · WITH THANKS:
John Adderley, Sâadane Afif, Jean Frémiot,
Vanessa Notley, Anna Selander, Brian R. Smith,
Penny Tyler · EDITED AT: Four Corners · DUBBED
BY: Warwick Sound · NEG CUT: Triad · PRINTED BY:
Rank Film Laboratories

Filmed on location in the sky above Lans en Vercors
Supported by École Nationale des Beaux-Arts de Bourges & Fonds Régional d'Art Contemporain du Centre

Disappearance at Sea 1996
16 mm colour anamorphic, optical sound,
14 minutes

CAMERA: John Adderley · SOUND TRANSFER: Steve Felton · WITH THANKS: Jamie Bennett, Pippa Coles, Helen Davidson, Ian Fairnington, Thomas Stewart · ANAMORPHIC LENS LOANED BY: Joe Duntan · EDITED AT: Four Corners · DUBBED BY: Warwick Sound · NEG CUT: Triad · PRINTED BY: Rank Film Laboratories
Filmed on location at St Abb's Head, Berwickshire · Made for *Berwick Ramparts Project* 1996

Delft Hydraulics 1996
16 mm black-and-white, optical sound,
3 minutes

CAMERA: Tacita Dean · SOUND ASSISTANTS: Esther Boender, Roland Groenenboom · SOUND TRANSFER: Steve Felton · EDITED AT: Four Corners · DUBBED BY: Studiosound · NEG CUT: Triad · PRINTED BY: Rank Film Laboratories
Filmed on location at Delft Hydraulics, De Voorst, The Netherlands

Foley Artist 1996
Laserdisc and monitor, eight speakers, Akai DR8 playback machine, Sondor magnetic playback machine, dubbing chart lightbox

ACTOR: Tim Pigott-Smith · FOLEY ARTISTS: Stan Fiferman, Beryl Mortimer · CAMERA: John Adderley · CLAPPER: Pip Laurenson ·

SOUND EDITOR: Martin Cantwell · TECHNICAL ADVISOR: Mike Dowson · PRODUCTION SUPERVISOR: Steve Felton · EDITOR: Rob Wright · SOUND POST PRODUCTION: The Sound Design Company · STILLS PHOTOGRAPHER: Stephen White · ON-LINE: Evolutions Television Ltd
Filmed on location at Delta sound, Shepperton Studios · Made for *Art Now*, Tate Gallery, London

Disappearance at Sea II 1997
16 mm colour anamorphic, optical sound,
1 minutes

CAMERA: John Adderley · LIGHTHOUSE MUSIC: Ian Stonehouse · SOUND TRANSFER: Steve Felton · WITH THANKS: Jamie Bennett, Pippa Coles, Helen Davidson, Ian Fairnington, Thomas Stewart · ANAMORPHIC LENS LOANED BY: Joe Duntan · EDITED AT: Four Corners · DUBBED BY: Warwick Sound · NEG CUT: Triad · PRINTED BY: Colour Film Services
Filmed on location at the Longstone Lighthouse, Farne Islands, Northumberland

Trying to Find the Spiral Jetty 1997
Audio CD, 27 minutes

WITH: Tacita Dean, Gregory Sax · SOUND EDITOR: Tacita Dean · DIGITAL SOUND POST PRODUCTION: The Sound Design Company · WITH THANKS: Steve Felton, Sandra Portman
Recorded on location at Rozel Point, Great Salt Lake, Utah

The Structure of Ice 1997
16 mm colour, optical sound, voice-over,
3 minutes

CAMERA: John Adderley · CAMERA ASSISTANT: Sam McCourt · SOUND TRANSFER: Steve Felton · WITH THANKS: Clare Cumberlidge, Rhona Garvin, Peter Morris, Nicola Perrin · EDITED AT: Four Corners

DUBBED BY: Warwick Sound · NEG CUT: Triad
PRINTED BY: Colour Film Services
Filmed on location at Blythe House, London
Made for *The Challenge of Materials Gallery*,
Science Museum, London

Gellért 1998
16 mm colour, optical sound, 6 minutes

CAMERA: Tacita Dean · ASSISTANTS: Heidi
Kellokoski, Fatime Plótár, Márta Radnóti, Sabina
Lang · SOUND TRANSFER: Steve Felton · WITH
THANKS: John Adderley, Barnabas Bencsik,
Mathew Hale, Pip Laurenson · EDITED AT: Four
Corners · DUBBED BY: Worldwide Sound · NEG CUT:
Triad · PRINTED BY: Colour Film Services
Filmed on location at the Gellért Baths, Budapest,
Hungary Made during the *In and Out of Touch*
London / Budapest Exchange Programme

Bubble House 1999
16 mm colour, optical sound, 7 minutes

CAMERA: Tacita Dean · ASSISTANT: Kjetil Berge ·
SOUND TRANSFER: Four Corners · WITH THANKS:
John Adderley · EDITED AT: Four Corners ·
DUBBED BY: Worldwide Sound · OPTICAL SOUND
TRANSFER: Martin Sawyer Sound Services ·
NEG CUT: TKT Film Services · PRINTED BY:
Metrocolour
Filmed on location on Cayman Brac

Sound Mirrors 1999
16 mm black-and-white, optical sound,
7 minutes

CAMERA: Tacita Dean · ASSISTANTS: Mathew Hale,
Maya Orme, Myles Orme, Ryan Orme · SOUND EDI-
TOR: Paul Hill · DIGITAL SOUND POST PRODUCTION:
Wexner Center Media Arts Program
WITH THANKS: John Adderley, Steve Felton, Julie

Crow · EDITED AT: Four Corners · OPTICAL SOUND
TRANSFER: Martin Sawyer Sound Services · NEG
CUT: TKT Film Services · PRINTED BY: Metrocolour
Filmed on location at Denge Sound Mirrors in Kent
Made for the Public Art Development Trust
Fourth Wall Project, The National Theatre,
London

**From Columbus, Ohio to the Partially Buried
Woodshed** 1999
Video, colour with sound, 9 minutes

WITH: Tacita Dean, Paul Hill, Maria Troy
CAMERA: Paul Hill · EDITOR: Paul Hill · POST
PRODUCTION: Wexner Center Media Arts Program
Filmed on location on or near the site of Robert
Smithson's *Partially Buried Woodshed*
Film of *Partially Buried Woodshed* (1970):
Collection Wexner Center for the Arts,
The Ohio State University, Columbus, Ohio, Gift
of Robert Swick · FILMED BY: Leonard Henzel
and Robert Swick Supported by Wexner Center
Media Arts Program, The Ohio State University

Banewl 1999
16 mm colour anamorphic, optical sound,
63 minutes

ASSISTANT DIRECTOR: Mathew Hale · DIRECTOR OF
PHOTOGRAPHY: John Adderley · CAMERA OPERATORS:
Jamie Cairney, Nick · MacRae, Tom Wright ·
CLAPPER LOADERS: Chris Connatty, Sam McCourt ·
SUN TRACKING MOTION CONTROL: Michael Geissler,
Lucien Kennedy-Lamb, Mark Seaton from
Tronbrook Ltd · ANAMORPHIC LENSES LOANED BY:
Joe Duntan, with thanks to Mason Cardiff · ARRI-
FLEX LOANED BY: Arri GB Ltd, WITH THANKS TO:
Alan Fyfe · ACL CAMERA AND MAGAZINES LOANED
BY: Graeme Stubbings and Simon Surtees · SOUND
RECORDISTS: Camden Logan, Sara Sender · DIGITAL

SOUND POST PRODUCTION: The Sound Design
Company · SOUND EDITOR: James Harrison · RUN-
NERS: Katy English, Rose Lord, Emily Whittle ·
PINHOLE RESEARCH AND STILLS PHOTOGRAPHY:
Richard Torchia · ECLIPSE PHOTOGRAPHY CONSUL-
TANT: Francisco Diego · CATERING: Katy English ·
BARBECUE: Blaise Vasseur, Lewis Horsman · WITH
THANKS TO: Emma Tod and Guy Waddell, Angela
Adderley, Steve Felton, Anya Gallaccio, Martyn
Ridgewell · WITH SPECIAL THANKS TO: Norman
Truscott, the cowman; Andrew Marment and
Roger Eddy for the loan of the cockerels; Ian
Stuart for his advice on local weather, Blue and
David and Helen Hosking for helping us film
Burnewhall Farm and their Pengwarnon Herd
of Pedigree Holstein Friesians · EDITED AT: Four
Corners · NEG CUT: TKT Film Services · OPTICAL
SOUND TRANSFER: Martin Sawyer Sound Services
PRINTED BY: Metrocolour · ORIGINATED ON: Kodak
Motion Picture Film
Filmed during the total eclipse of the sun
on Burnewhall Farm, St Buryan, Cornwall,
August 11th, 1999
Commissioned by St Ives International
for *As Dark As Light* 1999 with thanks
to Katy Sender
Supported by The National Lottery through The
Arts Council of England; Visual Arts Department
of the Arts Council of England; South West Arts,
South West Media Development Agency, Elephant
Trust, Henry Moore Foundation, Frith Street
Gallery, London,
Marian Goodman Gallery, New York

Friday / Saturday 1999

Akai DD8 Digital Dubber, 8 ARX
Climate 6s, Speakers, Wharton Timecode
Generator, MSF Radio Receiver synched to
the Rugby, Atomic Clock, four 18 Gbyte Rorke
Data Disk drives, eight 24 hour soundtracks,
eight description panels
SOUND RECORDINGS: Julie Crowe, Tacita Dean,
Steve Felton, Mathew Hale, Christina McBride,
Craig Peacock · SOUND EDITOR: James Harrison
Digital Sound · POST PRODUCTION: The Sound
Design Company · SYSTEM DESIGN: Feltech
Electronics Ltd, with thanks to Guy Gampell ·
SIGNWRITER: Danny Rogers of Studioart · WITH
THANKS: Andrea Schlieker
Sound recorded on location in Greenwich,
England; Ubatuba, Brazil; New Orleans, U.S.A.;
Hoonah, Alaska; Naselesele, Fiji; Akashi, Japan;
Dhaka, Bangladesh; Aden, Yemen
Commissioned by the New Millennium
Experience Company as part of *The North
Meadows Project*, Millennium Dome, London

Teignmouth Electron 2000

16 mm colour, optical sound, 7 minutes

CAMERA: Tacita Dean · ASSISTANT: Kjetil Berge ·
SOUND EDITOR: James Harrison · DIGITAL SOUND
POST PRODUCTION: The Sound Design Company ·
WITH THANKS: John Adderley, Steve Felton, David
Spence, National Maritime Museum, Greenwich ·
EDITED AT: Four Corners · DUBBED BY: Worldwide
Sound · OPTICAL SOUND TRANSFER: Martin Sawyer
Sound Services · NEG CUT: TKT Film Services ·
PRINTED BY: Metrocolour
Filmed on location on Cayman Brac

Totality 2000

16 mm colour anamorphic, mute,
11 minutes

CAMERA: John Adderley · CLAPPER LOADER: Chris
Connatty · SUN TRACKING MOTION CONTROL: Michael
Geissler, Lucien Kennedy-Lamb, Mark Seaton
from Tronbrook Ltd · ANAMORPHIC LENSES LOANED

BY: Joe Duntan, with thanks to Mason Cardiff ·
Arriflex loaned by Arri GB Ltd with thanks to
Alan Fyfe · ACL CAMERA AND MAGAZINES LOANED
BY: Graeme · Stubbings and Simon Surtees
EDITED AT: Four Corners · NEG CUT: TKT Film
Services · PRINTED BY: Metrocolour
Originated on Kodak Motion Picture Film
Filmed during the Total Eclipse of the Sun
on Burnewhall Farm, St Buryan, Cornwall,
August 11th, 1999

Jukebox 1 2000
1 console; 3 CD changing mechanisms;
192 CDs; 4 speakers

PROJECT MANAGER: Michael Geissler from
Tronbrook Ltd · DIGITAL SOUND POST PRODUCTION
MANAGER: Steve Felton from The Sound Design
Co. · DIGITAL SOUND POST PRODUCTION: James
Harrison from The Sound Design Co. · ELEC-
TRONICS & PROGRAMMING: Stuart Willcocks from
Tronbrook Ltd · CONSOLE DESIGN & FABRICATION:
Gary Hudson · CONTROL PANEL DESIGN: Mathew
Hale with Society · CONTROL PANEL FABRICATION:
K2 and Hamar Acrylic · CD PLAYER MECHANISM:
Sound Leisure Ltd

Jukebox 2 2001
1 console; 3 CD changing mechanisms;
192 CDs; 4 speakers

DIGITAL SOUND POST PRODUCTION MANAGER: Steve
Felton from The Sound Design Co. · DIGITAL SOUND
POST PRODUCTION: James Harrison from The Sound
Design Co. · ELECTRONICS & PROGRAMMING: Stuart
Willcocks · CONSOLE DESIGN & FABRICATION: Gary

Hudson · FABRICATION ASSISTANTS: Miles Speak,
Niall Stuckfield · CONTROL PANEL DESIGN: Mathew
Hale with Society · CONTROL PANEL FABRICATION:
K2 and Hamar Acrylic · CD PLAYER MECHANISM:
Sound Leisure Ltd · WITH THANKS: Michael
Geissler, Complete Fabrication · SUPPORTED BY:
Frith Street Gallery, London, Marian Goodman
Gallery, New York/Paris, Museu d'Art
Contemporani de Barcelona

Fernsehturm 2001
16mm colour anamorphic, optical sound,
44 minutes

ASSISTANT DIRECTOR: Mathew Hale · DIRECTOR OF
PHOTOGRAPHY: John Adderley · CAMERA OPERATORS:
Jamie Cairney, Tom Wright · CLAPPER LOADER:
Chris Connatty · ANAMORPHIC LENSES LOANED BY:
Joe Duntan · PROJECT CO-ORDINATOR: Friedrich
Meschede · LOCATIONS MANAGER: Rüdiger Lange ·
LOCATIONS ASSISTANT: Bettina Springer · WITH
THANKS: the staff and guests of the Fernsehturm
especially Herr Wellner, Heinz Schulz and Hans
Jurczik · KEYBOARD PLAYER: Jo Larisch · ADDI-
TIONAL GERMAN DIALOGUE: Karin Fiedler, Friedrich
Meschede · SOUND EDITOR: James Harrison ·
DIGITAL SOUND POST PRODUCTION: The Sound
Design Company with thanks to Steve Felton ·
EDITED AT: Thomas Geyer Filmproduktion ·
NEG CUT: TKT Film Services · PRINTED BY: Soho
Images
Originated on Kodak Motion Picture Film ·
SUPPORTED BY: Tate Britain, London; Frith Street
Gallery, London; Marian Goodman Gallery, New
York/Paris; Berliner Künstlerprogramm/DAAD

BIOGRAPHY

Solo exhibitions

1994
The Martyrdom of St Agatha and Other Stories,
Galerija Skuc, Ljubljana & Umetnostna Galerija,
Maribor (Slovenia)

1995
Clear Sky, Upper Air, Frith Street Gallery, London
Galerie "La Box", Ecole Nationale des Beaux
Arts, Bourges, France

1996
Foley Artist, ART NOW, Tate Gallery, London

1997
Tacita Dean, Witte de With Center for Contemporary Art, Rotterdam

The Drawing Room, The Drawing Center,
New York

Tacita Dean, Frith Street Gallery, London

1998
Galerie Gebauer, Berlin

Statements, Frith Street Gallery, Art Basel '98
De Pont Foundation, Tilburg, The Netherlands

Tacita Dean, ICA Philadelphia

1999
Tacita Dean, Madison Art Center, Wisconsin

Tacita Dean, Sadler's Wells, London

Marian Goodman Gallery, Paris

Tacita Dean, Cranbrook Museum

The Sea, with a Ship; Afterwards an Island,

Dundee Contemporary Arts, Scotland

Banewl, Newlyn Art Gallery, Penzance, Cornwall

Millennium Sculpture Project, The Millennium
Dome, London, 1999

2000
Marian Goodman Gallery, New York

Museum für Gegenwartskunst, Basel

Sala Montcada de la Fundació "la Caixa",
Barcelona

Art Gallery of York University, Toronto

Banewl, Matrix Program, Berkeley Art Museum,
University of California

Selected group exhibitions

1992
BT New Contemporaries, Newlyn Orion,
Penzance; Cornerhouse, Manchester

Orpheus Gallery, Belfast

Angel Row & The Bonnington, Nottingham;

Institute for Contemporary Art, London

1993
Barclays Young Artist Award, Serpentine Gallery,
London

Peripheral States, Benjamin Rhodes Gallery,
London

1994
Watt, Witte de With & Kunsthal, Rotterdam

Coming Up for Air, 144 Charing Cross Road &
the agency, London

Mise en Scène, Institute of Contemporary Arts,
London

1995

Mysterium Alltag, Hammoniale der Frauen,
Kampnagel, Hamburg, Germany

Kine[kunst]'95, Casino Knokke, Belgium

Video Forum, Art Basel 95, Switzerland

Speaking of Sofas, London Electronic Arts,
London Filmakers Co-op

Whistling Women, curated by Sarah Kent, Royal
Festival Hall, London

Videos and Films by Artists, Ateliers d'Artistes
de la ville de Marseille, France

British Art Show 4 , Manchester, Edinburgh &
Cardiff

Cubitt Street Gallery, London

1996

CCATV, Centre for Contemporary Art, Glasgow

Art Node Foundation, Stockholm

State of Mind, Centrum Beeldende Kunst,
Rotterdam

Swinging the Lead, International Festival of
the Sea, Bristol

Berwick Ramparts Project, Berwick upon Tweed,
Northumberland

Container '96, Copenhagen

Tacita Dean & *Stephen Wilks,* Galerie Paul
Andriesse, Amsterdam

Found Footage, Klemens Gasser & Tanja Grunert,
Cologne

1997

International Film Festival, Rotterdam

Challenge of Materials, Science Museum, London

A Case for a Collection, Towner Art Gallery,
Eastbourne

*Contemporary British Drawings - Marks &
Traces,* Sandra Gering Gallery, New York

Celluloid Cave, Thread Waxing Space, New York

Speaking of Sofas, Atheneum, Dijon, France

Flexible, Museum für Gegenwartskunst, Zurich

The frame of time – Openmuseum, Museum van
Hedendaagse Kunst, Limburg

Screenwriters Lab, Sundance Institute, Utah

At One Remove Henry Moore Institute, Leeds

20:20, Marian Goodman Gallery, New York

Social Space (curated by Dan Graham), Marian
Goodman Gallery, Paris

New Found Landscape, Kerlin Gallery, Dublin

1998

Voiceover: Sound and Vision in Recent Art,
National Touring Exhibition; Arnolfini, Bristol;
Hatton Gallery, Newcastle; Castle Museum,
Nottingham

*Wounds: Between Democracy and Redemption
in Contemporary Art,* Moderna Museet, Sweden

A - Z The Approach Gallery, London

Video / Projection / Film, Frith Street Gallery,
London

La Terre est ronde - Nouvelle narration, Musèe
de Rochechouart, France

La Mer n'est pas la Terre, FRAC Bretagne,
France

Disrupting the Scene, Cambridge Darkroom

Breaking Ground, Marian Goodman Gallery,
New York

Felsenvilla, Baden, Austria

The Turner Prize, Tate Gallery, London

1999

New Media Projects, Orchard Gallery, Derry, Northern Ireland

1264-1999 Une Lègende a Suivre,

Le Credac, Ivry, France

Appliance of Science, Frith Street Gallery, London

Hot Air, Granship, Convention and Arts Center, Japan

Marian Goodman Gallery, Paris

Geschichten des Augenblicks (Moments in Time), Kunstbau, Lenbachhaus, Munich

Go Away, Royal College of Art, London

New Visions of the Sea, National Maritime Museum, London

Fourth Wall, Public Art Development Trust at the Royal National Theatre, London

0 TO 60 IN 10 YEARS, Frith Street Gallery, London

Laboratorium, Antwerpen Open, Antwerp

Un monde rèel, Fondation Cartier, Paris

Tacita Dean, Lee Ranaldo, Robert Smithson, Dia Center for the Arts, New York

2000

Landscape, ACC Gallery, Weimar

The Sea and the Sky, Beaver College Art Gallery, Philadelphia

L'ombra della ragione, Galleria d'Arte Moderna Bologna

On the Edge of the Western World, Yerba Buena Center for the Arts, San Francisco

Von Edgar Degas bis Gerhard Richter: Werke auf Papier aus der Sammlung des Kunstmuseums Winterthur, Switzerland

Amateur/Liebhaber, Kunstmuseum, Kunsthallen & Hasselblad, Gothenberg, Sweden

Mixing Memory and Desire, neues Kunstmuseum Luzern

Artifice, Deste Foundation, Athens, Greece

The Sea and the Sky, Royal Hibernian Academy, Dublin

Another Place, Tramway, Glasgow

New British Art 2000: Intelligence, Tate Gallery, London

Somewhere near Vada (curated by Jaki Irvine), Project Art Centre, Dublin

media_city Seoul 2000, Seoul Metropolitan Museum

Tout le temps, La Biennale de Montreal

Vision and Reality, Louisiana Museum of Art, Denmark

BIBLIOGRAPHY

Selected books and catalogues

1992

BT New Contemporaries. Penzance: Newlyn
Orion; Manchester: Cornerhouse; Belfast: Orpheus
Gallery; Nottingham: Angel Row & The
Bonnington; London: Institute for Contemporary
Art, 1992.

1993

Barclays Young Artist Award. London: Serpentine
Gallery, 1993.

1994

Cahier No. 2. Rotterdam: Witte de With, 1994.

Mise en Scène. London: Institute for
Contemporary Art, 1994.

1995

British Art Show 4. London: National Touring
Exhibitions, Hayward Gallery, 1996.

Directory of British Film and Video Artists.
London: Arts Council of England, 1995.

General Release: Young British Artists at Scuola
di San Pasquale. Venice Biennale. Catalogue of
the exhibition with a project by Tacita Dean,
"Clover, 1995" (pp 68-69). 1995.

Mysterium Alltag. Hamburg, 1995.

Tacita Dean. Bourges: Ecole Nationale des
Beaux-Arts de Bourges, 1995.

1996

Berwick Ramparts Project. Berwick upon Tweed,
Northumberland, 1996.

1997

"Tacita Dean", Parkett, no. 50-51, 1997. Insert
with "Blackboard Drawings".

At One Remove. Leeds: Henry Moore Institute,
1997.

Cahier No 6. Rotterdam: Witte de With, 1997.

Disappearance at Sea. Limoges: Edition Adelie,
Bourges: L'Ecole Nationale de Bourges, 1997.
Signed edition of 100 copies.

Missing Narratives. Rotterdam: Witte de With,
1997. Extract from Cahier No. 6, printed in a
limited edition of 500 copies.

1998

Cahier No. 7. Rotterdam: Witte de With, 1998.

Cream: Contemporary Art in Culture, London:
Phaidon Press, 1998.

Nat West Art Prize 1998. London: Nat West
Group Art Collection, 1998.

Tacita Dean. Philadelphia: Institute of
Contemporary Art, University of Pennsylvania,
1998.

Voiceover: Sound and Vision in Current Art.
London: National Touring Exhibitions, South
Bank Centre, 1998.

Wounds: Between Democracy and Redemption in
Contemporary Art. Stockholm: Moderna Museet,
1998.

1999

From A to B and Back Again. London: Pale Green Press, 1999. (Published on occasion of the exhibition *Go Away: Artists and Travel*, Royal College of Art Galleries, 1999.)

Hot Air Granship. Tokyo, 1999.

Teignmouth Electron. Greenwich: Book Works in association with the National Maritime Museum, 1999.

2000

Amateur/Liebhaber. Gothenberg: Kunstmuseum, Kunsthallen & Hasselblad, 2000.

Artifice. London: The British Council, 2000.

Intelligence: New British Art 2000. London: Tate Britain, 2000.

Landscape. London: The British Council, 2000.

L'ombra della ragione. Bologna: La Galleria d'Arte Moderna, 2000.

media_city Seoul 2000. Seoul: Seoul Metropolitan Museum, 2000.

Mixing Memory and Desire. Luzerne: neues Kunstmuseum, 2000.

Somewhere Near Vada. Dublin: Project Art Centre, 2000.

Tacita Dean. Basel: Museum für Gegenwartskunst, 2000.

The Sea and the Sky. Philadelphia: Beaver College Art Gallery, Dublin: Royal Hibernian Academy, 2000.

Vision and Reality. Louisiana: Louisiana Museum of Art, 2000.

Selected articles and reviews

1993

Jacobs, Ulla, "Best of British: Idol", *Wiener Magazine*, April 1993.

Phillips, Andrea, "BT New Contemporaries, Barclays Young Artist Award Exhibition", *Hybrid Magazine* (London), no. 2, April-May 1993.

Thrift, Julia, "Beards, Breasts and Bloody Bodies", *The Guardian* (London), 22 January 1993.

1994

Cork, Richard, "Pioneer with a Gender Agenda", *The Times* (London), 15 November 1994.

Grant, Simon, "Coming up for Air", *Art Monthly* (London) May 1994.

Hubbard, Sue, "Tim Head and Tacita Dean", *Time Out Magazine* (London), 21 – 28 June 1994.

Jeffrey, Ian, "Art - Charades", *The London Magazine* (London), June-July 1994.

Kent, Sarah; "Role Call", *Time Out* (London), 26 October - 2 November 1994.

Lillington, David; "Coming up for Air", *Time Out* (London), March 23-30 1994.

Searle, Adrian, "Behind the Mask", *The Independent* (London), 25 October 1994.

Van den Boogerd, Dominic; "It's Real, but Very Fucked Up", *Metropolis M* (Amsterdam), no. 2, 1994.

1995

Anson, Libby, "Tim Head - Tacita Dean", *Art Monthly* (London), no. 188, July-August 1995.

Cork, Richard; "Tim Head and Tacita Dean", *The Times* (London), 27 May 1995.

Deepwell, Katy; "Uncanny Resemblances", *Women's Art Journal* (London), no. 62, January-February 1995.

Hunt, Ian, "Mise en Scene", *Frieze* (London), January-February 1995.

Irvine, Jaki, "Mise en Scene", *Third Text*, no. 30, spring 1995.

Schiff, Hajo, "Elefantendung und die Brüste der Agathe", *Inhalt*, March 1995.

1996

Cork, Richard, "Out with a chop, whir and clunk", *The Times* (London), 3 September 1996.

Feldman, Melissa E, "Foley Artist", *Art Monthly* (London), October 1996.

Greenberg, Sarah, "Art Now: Tacita Dean - Focus on New Art", *Tate Magazine* (London), no. 10, winter 1996-1997.

Greenberg, Sarah, "Berwick Ramparts Project", *Art Monthly* (London), September 1996.

Higgie, Jennifer, "Tacita Dean: Tate Gallery, London", *Frieze* (London), no. 31, November-December 1996.

Jones, Jonathan, "Tacita Dean: Tate Gallery, London", *Untitled*, no. 12, winter 1996.

Kent, Sarah; "Sound Gallery" preview, *Time Out* (London), 26 August - 3 September 1996

Lillington, David, "Foley Artist, Tate Gallery, London", *Metropolis M* (Amsterdam), no. 5, October 1996.

Lütticken, Sven, "Borsten van Sint Agatha", *Het Parool* (Amsterdam), 2 August 1996.

Sarah Greenberg, "Art Now: Tacita Dean", *Tate Magazine* (London), no. 10, winter 1996-1997.

Searle, Adrian, "Noises Off", Visual arts, *The Guardian* (London), 27 August 1996, p. 9

Süto, W., "De borsten van de heilige Agatha", *De Volkskrant* (Amsterdam), 30 August 1996.

Swenson, Ingrid, "A Lighthouse and Some Tapdancing: All in a Day's Work", *MAKE: The Magazine of Women's Art*, no. 72, October-November 1996.

1997

"Reward of Visiting Uptown Galleries", *The New York Times* (New York), 28 November 1997.

"Tacita Dean", *Time Out* (London), 24 September - 1 October 1997.

Dean, Tacita, "Zen and the Art of Film Making", *The Guardian*, 15 October 1997.

Del Re, Gianmarco, "Tacita Dean: Tate Gallery", *Flash Art*, May-June, 1997.

Ebner, Jörn, "Aus Frankensteins Genlabor", *Frankfurter Allgemeine Zeitung* (Frankfurt), 18 October 1997.

Richard, Frances, "Tacita Dean, The Drawing Room", *Artforum* (New York), November 1997.

Smith, Roberta, "The Celluloid Cave", *The New York Times* (New York), 27 June 1997.

1998

"Tacita Dean", *ID* (London), October 1998.

Brownrigg, Silvia, "Interview with a Dead Deceiver", *Frieze* (London), March - April 1998.

Cork, Richard, "Canvassing our Brightest Talent", *The Times* (London), 17 June 1998.

Currah, Mark, "Video, Projection, Film", *Time Out* (London), 10 – 17 June 1998.

Del Re, Gianmarco, "Cinema and the Sublime", *Contemporary Visual Arts*, no. 19, 1998.

Hopkin, Alannah, "New Found Landscape",

The Sunday Times (London), 4 January 1998.

Jeffett, William, "Tacita Dean", *Contemporary Visual Arts*, no. 17, 1998.

Lubbock, Tom, "Everyone's a Winner", *The Independent* (London), 3 November 1998.

McEwen, John, "Symbols and Enigmas", *The Sunday Telegraph* (London), 6 December 1998.

Walsh, Maria, "Beyond the Lighthouse: A Reflection on Two Films by Tacita Dean", *Coil Magazine*, no. 6, 1998.

1999

Buck, Louisa, "Prize Fighters", *Times Magazine* (London), 24 October 1999.

Colin, Beatrice, "Chalk One up for Light Fantastic", *Sunday Times Scotland*, 19 September 1999.

Cork, Richard, "Before a Show, See a Show - Richard Cork Applauds the Sadler's Wells Initiative in Commissioning Foyer Exhibitions", *The Times* (London), 5 May 1999.

Darwent, Charles, "Made for TV", *New Statesman*, 13 November 1999.

Di Folco, John, "Sou'westers at the Ready in Dundee", *Artwork*, October - November 1999.

Jeffrey, Moira, "Storm Drawing In", *Sunday Herald*, 12 September 1999.

Jones, Jonathan, "Is That a Joke", *The Guardian* (London), 4 November 1999.

Mahoney, Elisabeth, "Storm Warning", *Scotland on Sunday*, 12 September 1999.

Mahoney, Elisabeth, "Romance of the Sea", *The Guardian* (London), 23 September 1999.

Russel Taylor, John, "The Big Show - Tacita Dean", *The Times (Metro)* (London), 23 October 1999.

Schwabsky, Barry, "The Art of Tacita Dean", *Artforum* (New York), March 1999.

Thompson, Martin, "Misfit Lost in Time and Space (Martin Thompson meets T. Dean and Donald Crowhurst's son)", *The Sunday Telegraph* (London), 28 March 1999.

Turner, Jenney, "The Young Woman and the Sea", *The Independent* (London), 1 November 1999.

Walsh, Maria, "Tacita Dean", *Art Monthly* (London), June 1999.

2000

Coleman, Nick, "The Wooster Street Mystery", *The Independent* (London), 18 March 2000.

Searle, Adrian, "Noises Off", *The Guardian* (London), 8 July 2000.

Smith, Roberta, "Tacita Dean and Maurizio Cattelan", *The New York Times* (New York), 17 March 2000.

ACKNOWLEDGEMENTS I would like to thank John Adderley, Steve Felton and Martyn Ridgewell for all their professional help over many years in the making of various works; Gary Hudson and Stuart Willcox for their energy and invention in the manufacture of "Jukebox 2"; Michael Geissler and Tronbrook Ltd for allowing me to go ahead with the idea in the first place; Dr Theodora Vischer and Heidi Naef for presenting my work so beautifully in the Museum fur Gegenwartskunst in Basel which formed the base for this show; Jane Hamlyn, Rose Lord, Johanna Wistrom and Dale McFarland from Frith Street Gallery, London for their dogged and inexhaustible help and support, especially over the last year; Marian Goodman, Agnes Faerobe and everyone at Marian Goodman Gallery, New York and Paris for their continued support; Manuel Borja-Villel and everyone at MACBA for presenting my work in Barcelona. I would especially like to thank Roland Groenenboom for his long-standing commitment to my work; for having such faith in me from the very beginning and for being such an insightful and canny curator which has been so important and so enabling to the development of my life as an artist. And finally I would like to thank Mathew Hale for his often brilliant suggestions and understanding of my work.   **Tacita Dean**

MACBA would like to thank the following individuals and institutions for their collaboration with the exhibition *Tacita Dean* as lenders, and/or by permitting us to show films that belong to their collections: ARC Musée d'Art Moderne de la Ville de Paris, France; Walter Bechtler Stiftung, Kuesnacht, Switzerland; British Council Collection, London, England; Collection of Gilberto Charpenel, Guadalajara, Mexico; De Pont Foundation for Contemporary Art, Tilburg, The Netherlands; FNAC, Paris, France; FRAC Bretagne, Châteaugiron, France; Eric Franck, London; Frith Street Gallery, London; Emanuel Hoffmann Foundation/Museum für Gegenwartskunst, Basel, Switzerland; Sammlung Goetz, Munich, Germany; Marian Goodman Gallery, New York/Paris; Ruth Mannes and Frederic Cooper, New York; Tate Britain, London; Towner Museum and Art Gallery, Eastbourne, England; Zellweger Luwa AG, Uster, Switzerland; and all other private collectors who wish to remain unknown.

All works courtesy of the artist,
Frith Street Gallery, London
and Marian Goodman Gallery,
New York / Paris

EXHIBITION

Project Director
Manuel J. Borja-Villel

Curator
Roland Groenenboom

Assistant
Aida Roger

Architect
Isabel Bachs

Installation
Mètode

CATALOGUE

Editors
Mela Dávila
Roland Groenenboom

Coordination
Anna Jiménez Jorquera

Editing
Brian Holmes

Graphic Design
Ramon Prat
Montse Sagarra

Production
Font i Prat, Ass.
Carmen Galán

Printing
Ingoprint S.A.

Distribution
ACTAR
Roca i Batlle, 2-4
08023 Barcelona
Tel. 93 418 77 59
Fax 93 418 67 07
info@actar-mail.com
www.actar.es

Museu d'Art
Contemporani de Barcelona
Plaça dels Àngels, 1
08001 Barcelona
Tel. 93 412 08 10
Fax 93 412 46 02
macba@macba.es
www.macba.es

This book has been published on
occasion of the exhibition *Tacita
Dean*, held at the Museu d'Art
Contemporani de Barcelona from
January 26 to March 25, 2001.
Tacita Dean's texts on pages 4, 12,
20, 24, 30, 32, 34, 42, 44 and 62
were first published in *Cahier* no. 6
(Rotterdam), Witte de With, 1997;
texts on pages 22, 52, 54, 60, 64,
70 and 75 were first published in
Teignmouth Electron, London:
Book Works in association with the
National Maritime Museum, 1999;
text on page 46 was first published
in *Tacita Dean. An Aside*, Basel:
Museum für Gegenwartskunst
Basel, 2000.

Cover and back cover: details from
Bubble House, 1999.